Michael Watts studied Experimental Psychology at Sussex University, graduating with honours in 1980. He is the author of *Graphology*, which was published in Great Britain (Virgin Books, 1991), USA (Simon and Schuster, 1992), and in Spain.

Since 1983 he has been using graphology in personnel selection for companies in England, Australia, the USA and the Far East. He also uses his psychology background, in combination with his graphological skills, for vocational guidance and psychotherapy, and specializes in the field of relationship counselling.

Michael Watts lectures in England, Sweden and the USA and in addition to numerous radio and television appearances, regularly contributes articles on graphology to magazines and newspapers worldwide.

ℒOVESCRIPT

WHAT HANDWRITING
REVEALS ABOUT
LOVE AND ROMANCE

MICHAEL WATTS, B.Sc.

ST. MARTIN'S GRIFFIN
NEW YORK

ISBN 0-312-14118-1

Contents

PART FIVE
_____
'What's the Score in Bed?'

Appendix

Acknowledgements

The author's grateful thanks are due to the following:

Mr Charles Hamilton and Fraser's Autograph Gallery for permission to use handwriting samples.

The Imperial War Museum for help and advice.

Zosia Rooney, for doodles.

What Handwriting Reveals About Love and Romance

Introduction

It is now well accepted, within the field of psychology as well as in other areas of personality assessment, that body movements and gestures can potentially tell us a great deal about hidden thoughts and emotions.

As we deal with one another in our daily lives, we are continuously reacting and responding to this non-verbal communication, transmitted via tiny movements of the eyes and face muscles, as well as larger motions of the hands and other body parts.

From virtually the moment we are born, long before language forms any part of our daily existence, we respond to the muscular tonus of our mother's face and torso, sensing almost instantly her current state of mind. Using this knowledge, we instinctively adapt our own facial expressions and other body gesticulations, to signal our needs and convey our feelings.

According to anthropologists, when man first inhabited the earth, long before the advent of linguistic comm- unication, expressive gesture and non-verbal vocalizations were probably the only means of social interaction. Even today, in certain cultures, gestures still comprise an absolutely indispensable part of the language: the Bubis of West Africa cannot talk in the dark because their speech relies so much on accompanying gestures, and the sign-language of the deaf and dumb is a further example of the important role that gesture plays in human society.

It should come as no great surprise to learn that this subtle, yet highly expressive, silent communication often reveals far more about our innermost thoughts and feelings than the words we speak. Indeed, it is an awareness of this

1

fact that causes so many people (for a variety of different reasons) to consciously censor, and even contrive, their posture, expressions and gesticulations in communication with others both at work and at home.

Possessing the skill to accurately read this 'body language' is therefore widely valued within the field of personnel recruitment, as well as in many other occupations that require advanced communication capabilities. Psychologists, social workers, psychotherapists and police all need to depend upon their ability to accurately perceive human nature, and in all these professions a sensitivity to the 'language' of the body is clearly of paramount importance.

One interesting observation that has been made by researchers in the field of non-verbal communication is that small, subtle movements are invariably a more reliable source of information than larger ones, because they are far more difficult to consciously control, or alter, for purposes of deception or concealment. An almost imperceptible shifting of someone's eyes, for example, can alert an experienced interviewer to the fact that he or she is lying.

The most revealing and intricate body language of all is, of course, handwriting; a chain of gestures consisting of hundreds of tiny, expressive body motions, 'frozen' on to paper, that to a graphologist are a visible expression of an individual's emotions, inner attitudes, physical nature and behaviour patterns.

Being the ultimate display of very subtle movement, it is without any doubt the most valid and dependable indicator of character; the highly complex and coordinated muscular activity that takes place during the act of writing makes it far less susceptible than other forms of expressive body gesture to censorship and manipulation.

When people write, they are leaving behind a pattern of

who they are, that is as unique to them as their thumbprints. In addition, unlike brief, transient body gestures, which often last only a fraction of a second, handwriting captures on permanent record even the tiniest of motions, which can then be interpreted at leisure.

Using the graphology in this book, you will be in a position to 'defrost' these tell-tale signs, and expose the total personality that lies behind. You will have access to a system of knowledge which has won the approval of such people as Einstein, Jung, Freud and Adler, and has achieved such widespread respect that it has long been included as a standard part of the psychology curriculum in several well-known universities.

A growing number of psychiatrists, psychologists, and others working in the field of psychotherapy and counselling, are turning to professional graphologists for a second opinion. This is sometimes the only way to reach an accurate diagnosis of clients who are extremely withdrawn or even silent. Such individuals are frequently unresponsive to more conventional methods of psychological evaluation, based upon answers to questions, and a discussion of problems, past and present. Also, graphologically monitoring a person's writing throughout a course of treatment can serve as a reliable barometer of their progress or deterioration.

One of graphology's numerous advantages over many other methods is that it cannot be misused by the prejudiced mind, for it is entirely a non-discriminatory technique, blind to race, religion and colour.

At this point, a question that is frequently posed by sceptics, is, 'If graphology is such an effective technique for assessing human nature, why has there not been considerably more scientific research into this system? Why is it only now, in this century, that there has been a real explosion of widespread interest directed towards this topic?'

There are two clear answers to this inquiry: firstly, before the turn of the twentieth century many people were illiterate. Consequently, there was little motivation to embark on a comprehensive research programme, in an area which at best could only provide knowledge of personality within a limited section of the population.

Secondly, graphology is a subsection of psychology, which lies within the field of social sciences. Extensive academic interest in this whole domain is very recent. It is interesting to note however, that in Europe (Switzerland and Germany in particular) graphology is amongst the oldest of the psychological approaches for studying personality; it was in use prior to the advent of psychoanalysis, Gestalt therapy, projective techniques and social anthropology.

Graphology is a technique of observation and interpretation, based upon classified knowledge which has been empirically collected, and developed into a science by a large number of highly qualified researchers. It is therefore far from being merely intuitive, although as with all the other social or behavioural sciences (and even in fields such as medicine), a developed intuition or 'sixth sense' is an extremely valuable asset.

Graphology is still, relatively speaking, in its early formative stage of development, and it has therefore had to accept its share of scepticism and criticism, as did many of today's respected professions when they were evolving (a notable example being psychiatry). As any such young profession develops, many of the former criticisms and doubts drop away, and fortunately the same is happening very rapidly within the field of graphology.

This book was inspired by letters from enthusiastic

readers of my previous work, and also by clients who have sought my counselling services to help them with their personal relationships. I was asked to write a book specializing in what is perhaps the most important area of handwriting analysis: relationships and compatibility.

In Great Britain, recent surveys have shown that one in four people lives alone (not out of choice), and one in three marriages ends in divorce. The statistics in many other countries around the world are similarly depressing. Using graphology to assess the personalities of several hundred couples, I have discovered that the root source of conflict and failure in this area can frequently be traced back to an unhappy sex life. The findings of numerous psychologists, and others specializing in relationship counselling, also support this view.

It seems that conflicts in a relationship are far easier to resolve if the couple concerned is sexually compatible. Conversely, when a couple is sexually incompatible, perception of conflict becomes distorted and magnified out of all proportion. Without using a knowledge of hand-writing analysis, sexual differences often remain undiscovered until it is too late. The excitement felt at the start of a relationship often camouflages any serious problems. As with my previous book, I have tried to avoid the use of graphological jargon, so the material should be easy to comprehend and use, even for the complete novice.

All the graphological material included in this book has been selected for its significance in yielding insight into the most important areas of personality. It should, therefore, prove an invaluable guide for those in search of a partner with a compatible sexual appetite. In addition, it will allow the reader to steer well clear of disturbed types who could, for example, turn out to be physically violent or emotionally sadistic.

Before You Begin Reading This Book

Make use of the blank boxes at the end of this section, so that you always have within easy reach those examples of writing you most wish to learn about.

If you are a complete novice to graphology, this will be your last chance to get a completely unbiased sample of your own handwriting. Once you have developed some knowledge of the subject this will inevitably cause you, consciously or subconsciously, to remove those aspects of writing style that reveal undesirable characteristics, and instead, you will begin to adopt more positive or complimentary handwriting features.

So before you begin reading this book, take a pen you enjoy writing with that suits your style, and while sitting relaxed and comfortably at a table or desk, use the box provided at the end of this section to permanently store a sample of your **natural** writing (the way you would write a letter, rather than a hurriedly written note). When you have done this, put your normal signature at the bottom. (The sample should not be produced if you are under the influence of alcohol, drugs, severe fatigue or illness.) The following sentences should be used for this purpose, as they contain all the letters of the alphabet, as well as some key capital letters.

I thought I saw the quick brown fox jumping over the lazy doggy, I looked again and then I saw that it was only foggy.

Wales and Monaco have a Prince, Norway and Thailand

6

have Kings, but there is no King in Hungary, Venezuela or Russia, as no Monarchy exists there.

Some people's script is always composed entirely of block capitals. If your writing is like this, then in addition to writing the above sentences in your normal style, you should also provide another sample in cursive writing.

If the size or style of your script makes it impossible for you to write the whole of the above sentences in the space provided, this is perfectly all right. Do not try to adapt your normal manner of writing to suit the available space, as whatever fits naturally into the box will be enough.

However, if your writing does fall into this category, you should write the sentences again, on a separate sheet of paper that allows you sufficient space (there will be the security of knowing that if you should mislay this loose sheet, you will still have some of your script permanently recorded in the book).

Even if your script does fit comfortably into the box provided, it is still always a good idea to keep at hand extra examples of your handwriting.

Something written spontaneously will do nicely (content is completely unimportant) as long as it is of sufficient length to include most of the letters of the alphabet, as well as some capitals. Alternatively, you may be able to get hold of some letters you have written fairly recently. Writing from the distant past, however, is not likely to be appropriate, as your personality may have significantly altered, and if so, the writing will not be a reflection of your current character and behaviour.

At this point, there will undoubtedly be some readers who will exclaim, 'But my writing is never the same from one day to the next, and it can even look different depending upon the time of day.'

Such readers can rest assured that there is nothing to worry about, for just as our thoughts and reactions are influenced by our current emotions, physical condition, and the particular demands of any given moment, so, too, is our handwriting.

From the viewpoint of handwriting analysis however, these changes pose no real problem, as the essence of an individual's personality and behaviour is derived from a large number of deeply rooted handwriting features and aspects of writing style that are not significantly altered by temporary changes of mood and environment.

What people are in fact observing, when they claim their handwriting looks completely different from day to day, is simply changes in superficial handwriting characteristics that reflect only peripheral or very minor components of personality, and not those central areas of human make-up that would influence the main body of a graphological analysis.

Even if people choose to purposely alter their writing in order to deceive a graphologist, they still only succeed in making very unimportant changes (from a graphological standpoint), which would alter the interpretation of merely insignificant features of personality and not those major areas comprising the real substance of a person's character and behaviour.

Once you have organized a sample of your own writing, then you should ask your partner, or any prospective partner, to provide a sample of their writing (following the same procedure as you used). This should also be stored in the relevant blank box on the following page.

You may wish to use the last remaining box for further samples of writing belonging to family, friends or any other personalities you feel you would like to learn more about.

As you read through this book, you will find yourself

continually referring back to this page with increasing fascination. The insight and knowledge you gain of yourself and others will considerably enrich your existence by helping you to reach an understanding of human nature that will enable you to accept your own and others' failings with more compassion.

If when you are examining a piece of writing you come across apparently incongruous aspects of character that are quite definitely at opposite ends of the spectrum, do not panic. This simply means that the individual concerned shifts from one pattern of behaviour to the other, depending upon circumstances in combination with his or her current state of mind.

For instance, in the same sample of writing you might find graphological signs indicating a low interest in sex, as well as signs which suggest a very strong interest in sex. This person will simply fluctuate between these two different extremes depending upon mood. The proportionate amount of time spent in one state or the other can easily be determined by comparing the frequency of appearance of the respective aspects of handwriting style revealing each of these two different behaviour patterns.

If the handwriting feature disclosing a strong interest in sex appears regularly, whereas the other feature is rare, this means that you are dealing with someone who has a strong sensual appetite, but who very occasionally slips into a state of mind where there is a complete lack of interest in lovemaking. In such instances it is clearly just a question of ascertaining the strength of the different writing features by measuring the frequency of appearance, and then one simply uses intelligent judgment to determine how often each behaviour pattern expresses itself.

You must always remember, however, to keep an open mind when you are using graphology. Sometimes you are bound to come across signs that disclose attributes of personality which you feel cannot possibly be true, with regards to the particular individual whose writing you are analyzing. There are several feasible explanations for this. You may simply possess a poor instinct for assessing human nature, or you may have had very little contact with the person, and if either of these possibilities is true, you should mistrust your personal opinion on the matter and rely upon the graphological interpretation.

Even if you claim to know the person very well, and have full confidence in your powers of perception, there is nevertheless a chance you might have discovered a side of this character that will only express itself in exceptionally intimate surroundings. Most people heavily censor what they show of themselves to others, and frequently even the best of friends will hide attributes they consider undesirable or highly personal.

Alternatively, an apparently incongruous characteristic may, in fact, be merely a latent potential or an unwanted trait that has been completely suppressed to the point where it is no longer an active component of the person's behaviour.

Be sure to remain objective at all times, and do not allow your personal biases or preconceived ideas to cloud your judgment or destroy your confidence in what you detect from your graphological analysis.

Also, while it is absolutely essential that you base your analyses on tried and tested graphological information, you should not neglect the use of intuition in the whole process.

If you allow it, this invaluable sixth sense will help you link together into a comprehensive portrait the aspects of character that have been derived from the fundamental graphological principles. In fact, the difference between a mediocre and an excellent graphological analysis is frequently determined by the skill with which one can utilize intuition in bringing to life the various pieces of deduced personality, by combining them into a balanced, dynamic and complete picture of an individual's thoughts, feelings and behaviour.

One word of advice before you dive headlong into the exciting adventure awaiting you within the pages of this book. The way you use the graphological information is clearly your own responsibility. If it is used as a means to help yourself and others reach a deeper level of understanding and self-acceptance, then you really cannot go wrong. On the other hand, if you are foolish enough to exploit this newly found power malevolently, as a weapon to hurt, criticize or manipulate, you will surely create for yourself a great deal of 'bad *karma*' (a Buddhist term describing the phenomenon where one's own negative actions return, possibly in some other form, to haunt one at a later stage).

Finally, as a general rule, when you are analyzing someone's writing do not discuss his or her personality when other people can hear what you are saying, as this shows a lack of respect for feelings and privacy, and can cause a great deal of unnecessary discomfort and embarrassment. On a private, one-to-one basis, it is possible to be far more candid, and discuss, if requested (and not otherwise), less desirable areas of the character that may come to light. Also, make sure you remain continually aware of the person's emotional responses to what you are saying, and always try to be sympathetic and tactful. Certain things you may discover in someone's writing may be too personal to discuss, and are therefore better left unsaid.

Now you are ready to begin your adventure into the fascinating labyrinth of the human psyche. Have fun!

SAMPLE OF YOUR WRITING

SAMPLE OF YOUR PARTNER'S WRITING

OTHER SAMPLES OF WRITING

SEXUAL SELF-AWARENESS QUIZ

Do not turn to the end of this chapter to check your results until you have answered all the questions, otherwise your score will be biased.

Sexual self-awareness is obviously an essential requirement for anyone in search of a sexually satisfying relationship. You cannot expect to find the right person if you are not sure exactly what you are looking for, and to discover that you obviously first need to know a great deal about yourself.

By answering the following questions on your sexual nature, you will be able to get some idea of the accuracy of your present sexual self-awareness. In addition, you can test, as well as enhance, your knowledge of other people's sexual nature, by applying these same questions to them.

To check your answers, simply take a sample of your own (or if relevant, someone else's) handwriting, and turn to the end of the chapter, where you will be provided with answers based on an objective graphological assessment. If your sexual self-awareness is good, you should get full marks. If one answer is wrong, this is by no means drastic. If, however, two or more of your answers turn out to be incorrect, then your sexual self-awareness is definitely not good.

1. As compared with the general population, do you think your sexual imagination is
   a. extremely vivid *b.* average *c.* poor?

2. Is your capacity for sensual pleasure
   a. high *b.* medium or *c.* low?

3. Which of these three descriptions fits you best:
   a. sexually repressed *b.* sexually severely repressed *c.* neither of these?

4. If your lover did something to make you jealous, do you think you would feel
   a. only mild anger *b.* strong anger *c.* very intense anger?

5. If you were having an affair, would you find it
   a. very easy *b.* easy *c.* difficult to hide this from your partner?

HANDWRITING QUIZ

Test your current ability to interpret personality from handwriting by answering the following quiz on samples of script belonging to the famous and infamous.

If you already have some knowledge of handwriting analysis, you should not expect to get more than one wrong answer. If, however, you are completely new to handwriting analysis, you will discover whether or not you have a natural talent for deducing personality from writing. Absolute beginners who get only one wrong answer should consider making a serious study of graphology, for they have a good intuition for the subject. More than three wrong answers means you have very little genuine interest in graphology.

1. Which of these three famous women has a healthy sexual appetite as well as a very vivid sexual fantasy?

a.

b.

c.

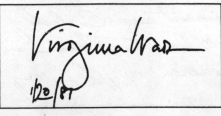

2. One of these renowned American males from the nineteenth century suffered from severe sexual repression. Which one?

a.

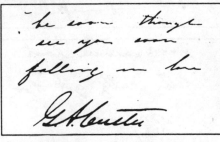

b.

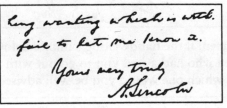

3. Which particular shape, appearing in both samples *a.* and *b.*, do you think signifies possible homosexual tendencies?

a.

b.

4. Which one is the violent rapist?

a.

b.

5. For women: if the handwriting samples below belonged to two men who had asked you to go out with them alone on a date, which one would you be well advised to refuse?

a.

b.

6. One of these well-known 'macho' males has a graphological sign in their writing which suggests latent homosexual tendencies. Which one?

a.

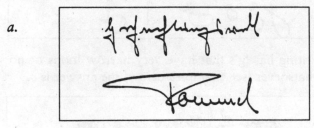

b.

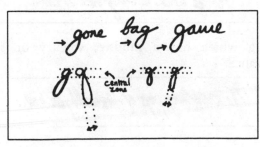

ANSWERS TO SEXUAL SELF-AWARENESS QUIZ

1. If the writing has two or more 'g's with a looped stem that is at least as wide as the central zone (see example below), the objective graphological answer is *b*.

If however the looped stems are twice as wide as the central zone (or more), the answer is *a*.

If the writing has 'g's that have very narrow loops or no loops whatsoever (see examples below) the answer is *c*.

2. If the writing has one of the characteristics below, then the answer is *b*. If it has more than one of them, the answer is *a*. If it has none of them, and in addition the writing was written by choice with a pen that has an extremely fine tip that produces sharp-looking writing the answer is *c*.

• Writing containing many letters that are clogged with ink.

• Writing which has a muddy, smeary or smudgy appearance.

- Writing done from choice with a thick, felt-tip pen, or any other pen producing broad, thick lines.

> ### feelings Awareness

- Writing where heavy pen pressure makes indentations that clearly show on the reverse of the paper.

3. If the writing has 'g's with stems that consistently have a very narrow loop (see example below) then the answer is *a*.

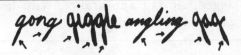

If the stems are consistently so narrow that many are retraced (see example below) then the answer is *b*.

If there are hardly any stems of the type shown above, then the answer is *c*.

4. If the writing has none of the characteristics below, the answer is *a*. If it has only one of the characteristics, the answer is *b*. If it has two or more of them, the answer is *c*.

- A restless, messy look, caused by an alternating slant, in combination with capital letters which are very large and showy, written with such heavy pen pressure that indentations can be clearly seen on the reverse of the paper.

- Most of the letters within words are joined together, leaning so far to the right that they appear to be falling over.

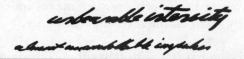

- Several examples of capital letters with a small circular attachment or a squared loop to the beginning of the letter.

- A very jagged, zig-zag appearance, with heavy pen pressure causing indentations.

/ am coming home now

5. If the writing has none of the characteristics below, the answer is *c*. If it has only one of the characteristics, the answer is *b*. If it has two or more of them, the answer is quite definitely *a*.

- Legible writing with words missing a whole letter or part of a letter (you need to find three or more examples). This does not apply to letters that are missing due to excessive speed of writing, or to the writing of dyslexics.

difficult thinking accident

- The small letter 'a', 'c', 'o' or 'g' made with a double or treble loop (check that there are several letters with this sign).

advance precisely look flag

- Writing with several examples of lines that have a wavy baseline.

sometimes I feel quite unsteady.

ANSWERS TO HANDWRITING QUIZ

1. The correct answer is sample *c*. The writer is Virginia Wade, the Wimbledon tennis champion. The gigantic balloon-shaped stem on the letter 'g' and the extremely long descending line on this same letter are indications of enormous sexual energy and an abundantly vivid sexual fantasy. (Sample *a*. was written by Marilyn Monroe, and sample *b*. by HM Queen Elizabeth II.)

2. The correct answer is sample *a*., which was written by General George A. Custer, the American Indian fighter.

(Sample *b.* was written by President Abraham Lincoln.) In Custer's writing, the loops on the stems of his letter 'g's are so narrow that many of them are retraced (i.e. the upstroke retraces the downstroke). This is a classic graphological indicator of severe sexual repression. It is interesting to note that many other famous historical figures known for their extreme dedication to their work (including many other prominent men of war) also have this same sign of sexual repression. Perhaps it is the sublimation of this immense (frustrated) sexual energy into their careers that results in their being such high achievers. (A female example of this trend is Madame Curie, the renowned scientist, whose writing consists almost entirely of retraced stems.)

3. The answer is the 'phallus-shaped' extensions, seen on the 'g' stem of the signature of Billie Jean King (the famous Wimbledon tennis champion, who claims to be a lesbian), and also in numerous places on lower stems in sample *b.* which was written by an eighteenth-century transvestite called Chevalier Eon De Beaumont who worked in Russia, for the French government, as a sort of spy. His transvestite behaviour was the inspiration for the word 'eonism', a synonym for transvestism.

4. The correct answer is sample *b.*, which was written by the evil and infamous Albert De Salvo, an American rapist and serial killer better known as 'The Boston Strangler'. The major graphological clue to this person's severely disturbed mind and violent nature is seen in the sudden and irregular heavy bursts of pressure throughout his writing.

If you chose sample *a.* you can be forgiven for this incorrect answer, as club-shaped lower stems (as seen in this writing) almost always signify very violent behaviour patterns. In certain rare cases however, people with this characteristic in their writing may have learnt to channel their aggressive tendencies in a socially acceptable manner. It is interesting to note, however, that this writing belongs to the former American attorney general Robert Kennedy, and there are many experts who believe that he was connected with several acts of violence, such as the attempted assassination of Fidel Castro (which may have led to his own death) and there are also strong suggestions that Marilyn Monroe was the victim of a murder plot in which Robert Kennedy was involved.

5. If you turned down sample *b.*, you definitely made the correct choice, as the writing belongs to the crazy, vicious American serial killer David Berkowitz, better known as 'Son of Sam'. As with the writing of 'The Boston Strangler' discussed above, the major graphological clue to this person's severely disturbed mind and violent nature is seen in the sudden and irregular heavy bursts of pressure on several words in the writing, e.g. 'Brooklyn'. Sample *a.* was written by a former American President, George Washington, and there are absolutely no visible negative graphological signs present in this writing.

6. Sample *a.* is the correct answer. It was written by the World War Two German Field Marshal, Erwin Rommel. Note the 'double-looped' lower stems on letters which resemble the numeral eight (the ascending line rises up first, on the right-hand side of the descending line, prior to moving to the left and back again to the right to form the second loop). This sign is a strong indicator of latent homosexual tendencies in the personality. This does not mean however that such inclinations will ever actually be

expressed, as such individuals may suppress them and choose instead to lead an entirely heterosexual lifestyle.

Sample *b.* was written by the author Ernest Hemingway.

PART ONE

The Alphabet of Sex and Relationship

1. Overview of the Alphabet

When faced with learning a new language it is always advisable (and traditional) to begin with its alphabet. The same rule applies to the process of learning graphology. Indeed, when the system of handwriting analysis first began it was based almost entirely on a graphology alphabet – the classification and interpretation of individual letter-shapes, and this remained the case for over fifty years. Later on in its evolution, handwriting analysis developed a more holistic approach that emphasized an assessment and interpretation of aspects of writing style that influence the whole writing process such as rhythm, organization, fluency, originality, size and slope of writing.

In the light of the relative complexity and subtlety of this new and much more in-depth, thorough approach to analysis, there arose an attitude of contempt and disrespect towards the old 'alphabet' system. Instead of acknowledging its many positive qualities, and intelligently synthesizing them with the new techniques, the first system was simply cast aside by a large number of handwriting analysts.

However, in spite of the enormous advances and improvements of modern graphology over the original 'letter-shape' approach, the graphology alphabet deserves a respected (though admittedly) secondary position within the system of handwriting analysis for a number of reasons.

To begin with, to understand and make use of the concepts and methods of the modern holistic approach, a considerable amount of time and effort needs to be devoted to study, and even after this, the process of analyzing writing is by no means instantaneous, as it requires following various procedures of measurement and careful assessment. The absolute beginner, using only the modern approach and ignoring the graphology alphabet, has little chance of ascertaining anything at all from someone's writing until these stages have been gone through.

The graphology alphabet, however, can be understood, assimilated, and applied to a piece of writing within a period of a few minutes. Unlike the holistic method, this system can be instantly utilized, even by a complete novice, as no prior learning is required. There is another great advantage with the graphology alphabet: it is a commonly known fact among students of graphology that one needs a decent-sized sample of someone's writing in order to achieve a thorough and complete understanding of the personality. Unfortunately it is not always possible to fulfil this ideal requirement, and there may be circumstances in which one is obliged to attempt an analysis of personality based upon a mere handful of words. Nothing even close to a comprehensive portrait could ever be derived from such a small sample, but if one chose to utilize the graphology alphabet, one could, nevertheless, potentially discover a few highly revealing characteristics that might influence an important decision, such as whether to develop a relationship with a partner who could turn out to be physically violent.

It seems obvious that one should respect not only the modern, holistic methods of graphology, but also the original system of the graphology alphabet. The ideal approach to handwriting analysis exists in a synthesis of the two techniques.

In this part of the book, you are provided with a thorough interpretation of all the letter-shapes which can potentially reveal aspects of a person's behaviour within the realms of an intimate relationship. Since the essential theme of the book is concerned with sex and relationship, the descriptions of personality given for each letter-shape are written with a major emphasis on the sexual and emotional relationship connotations of the sign, and do not include information concerning work habits, or other expressions of character not pertaining directly to this area.

Ideally the information in this chapter should be used in conjunction with the rest of the graphology in the book, in order to create a complete and comprehensive analysis. If, however, you have insufficient time for this, or are simply too impatient to embark upon this thorough approach, this alphabet will provide an extremely rapid and accurate (though incomplete) insight into a large number of important characteristics that play a significant role in determining the quality of feeling between two people.

Clear, precise, handwritten illustrations of each letter-shape are given together with the aspects of personality they reveal. Occasionally, if the letter-shape is especially revealing, the reader may be referred to other sections of the book for additional information.

Remember, when you are looking up the meaning of a particular letter-shape, that you should go through all the given variations for that particular letter of the alphabet, as sometimes several different variations can apply to the same letter. For instance, if the writing contains a 'g' which has a triangular-shaped stem and you want to look up the meaning of this triangle shape, do not stop when you match this up and discover the person is a domestic tyrant with a critical nature, but check onwards through the list of possible variations of 'g' where you may find further information, for example, the stem may also be very long which signifies enormous sexual energy.

Occasionally you may notice that a person shapes a particular letter of the alphabet in more than one way.

When you see this, note down the information on personality corresponding to each of these different variations, as all of it is relevant.

Usually when you are analyzing a piece of writing it is a good idea to note how the person shapes all the letters of the alphabet, then by looking up the corresponding meanings in the alphabet, you can build up a clear personality portrait. Some letters, however, are far more revealing than others, and it is useful to examine these first, especially if you are short of time. The most important small letters are the 'a', 'd', 'g', 'm' and 't'. When you have studied these, you should carefully look at the next chapter, 'Key Symbols'. These two steps will allow you to derive, very rapidly, a fair amount of information about someone's personality, on those occasions when you do not have the time to systematically go through all the chapters in this book.

Any given letter-shape in the chapter will apply to writing of any size or style, whether or not it is neat or legible. You need to spot a sign at least two or three times in a piece of writing in order to be sure that the corresponding personality description applies, and in certain cases a letter-shape will need to be seen several times, or even constantly repeated throughout a piece of writing, for it to be valid. Finally, all the descriptions of personality apply equally to men and women unless otherwise specified.

2. Key Symbols

SYMBOLIC SHAPES THAT CAN APPEAR ON CAPITAL OR SMALL LETTERS

THE MINI-CIRCLE

Capital or small letters that have a small circular attachment:

malta Eva Gone fat seawit

This person is extremely jealous and possessive. He or she will be quick to notice any sign of infidelity. A glance or a word exchanged by a partner with a member of the opposite sex may be enough to trigger suspicion.

The effect of this on such a person's sex life will vary. Some may deal with the fear that a relationship is under threat by attempting to improve the quality of their lovemaking; others may react by becoming extremely angry and refusing to make love until an explanation of the supposed infidelity is given.

For detailed information on the sexual · behaviour patterns and other aspects of personality connected with this graphological characteristic, see 'The Jealous Lover', page 296.

THE PHALLUS

Capital or small letters which have a phallus shape:

$$BE\omega\mathcal{M}\mathcal{fp\varepsilon}$$

If you are looking for a partner with a conventional attitude to sex, give this one a miss! For this individual can achieve sexual satisfaction only when indulging in certain highly unorthodox practices.

Such people possess a vivid erotic fantasy, and their minds are filled with images of themselves gaining sexual pleasure in ways which many people would consider unacceptable.

If you are intending to begin an intimate relationship with this person, you should find out first exactly what his or her sexual preferences are, or you could be in for an unpleasant surprise unless your own tastes are similar.

For detailed information on the sexual behaviour patterns and other aspects of personality connected with this graphological characteristic, see 'I Wonder...Straight or Gay?', page 205.

THE EAGLE'S TALON

**Capital or small letters containing
an 'Eagle's Talon' formation:**

Jan Stan g dog y

This person suffers from feelings of guilt that are rooted in an unhealthy self-esteem, shaped by a disturbed, unhappy childhood.

Having a very animal-like attitude to existence, such people are extremely self-centred, and possess a scheming, calculating mind and an inwardly rebellious nature. They tend generally to switch off any sensitivity to other people's feelings and needs, and this, as well as various other anti-social characteristics in their personality, will make it very difficult for anyone to establish a long-lasting relationship with them.

They definitely do not relish taking care of the various duties and responsibilities that are a standard part of most serious relationships. Indeed, it will come as no surprise if they are skilful in coming up with all sorts of clever excuses in an attempt to extricate themselves from these obligations. It is therefore highly unlikely that people with this writing characteristic will make any significant effort to fulfil a partner's needs and desires, unless they are still trying to make a good impression in the early courtship stages of a relationship. If a partner begins to complain or becomes generally dissatisfied, they will use their skill in sensing vulnerable areas of the personality to subtly undermine his or her self-confidence and self-worth, so as to suppress any outspoken feelings of discontentment.

Perhaps due to a subconscious desire for punishment, to escape the earlier mentioned guilty feelings that are simmering in the deeper recesses of their minds, they have also developed a habit of continually provoking their partners into resenting them, by pointing out weaknesses in an insensitive and disparaging manner.

People who make an 'Eagle's Talon' formation on the lower stem of the letter 'g' will also be permanently dissatisfied with their sex lives, and it is very unlikely that they will rate highly as lovers. Obviously, the general disharmony and conflict such people create in relationships will be largely to blame for this, but another contributing factor will be their unconventional sexual tastes. Finding a mate with a similar sexual appetite, who will be willing to satisfy their unusual lusts, will not always be easy.

Men with this graphological characteristic may enjoy sexual activities that most women would find somewhat perverse, and they are frequently prone to deceitfulness, so one certainly could not guarantee their fidelity in a monogamous relationship.

If this graphological characteristic appears on the lower stem of the letter 'y', then during childhood, as a result of great emotional suffering or feelings of material deprivation, the writer has developed a strongly acquisitive streak. Such people will be unusually possessive of personal belongings, and very tight-fisted.

On the positive side, their partners can rest assured that one way or another, they will manage to provide for an economically secure life, as they have a cunning eye for viable financial opportunities, and will not be averse to adopting unorthodox approaches, or bending the rules, in order to overcome any hurdles that stand in their way.

THE WAVE AND THE SMILE

**Capital or small letters that have a
wavy line or a 'smile' line:**

m̃H́T Ɉ p n t̃ ĩ m w

If you are the type of person who considers humour to be an indispensable requirement in an intimate relationship, then you will certainly be starting off on a good note if you have just begun dating someone who has this graphological characteristic.

People who form 'Waves' or 'Smiles' as they write have a good ability to see the funny side of existence, so when the atmosphere gets stressful they are sometimes able to transmute their own and other people's tension into laughter, with the help of some well-chosen humorous comment or joke.

This should prove a valuable asset, as it will help them to achieve a generally smooth level of communication in relationships. In addition, their light-hearted manner will boost the quality of their sex life, for laughter stimulates endorphins – 'pleasure chemicals' which relax the body, and enhance the enjoyment of all sensual activities.

For a complete explanation of this physiological phenomenon, as well as a detailed explanation of other aspects of personality and sexual behaviour associated with these graphological indicators, see 'The Humorous Lover', page 268.

THE LONG STICK

Capital or small letters with a rigid diagonal line attached, that starts from clearly below the baseline:

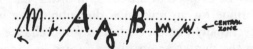

If you are an understanding type, and find it easy to pardon a loved one who has showered you with verbal abuse during a moment of stress, then this person is your exact opposite.

When such people are wronged, they will certainly not just 'forgive and forget', as they have a marked tendency to bear grudges. They nurture grievances far too long, and will remember even the minor details of occasions when they have been hurt in some way.

Such behaviour almost certainly has roots which stretch back far into their past, to a time when they developed feelings of bitterness and resentment towards a particular person or situation that caused them, or maybe someone they cared about, much suffering.

If the diagonal line starts from well below the base of the letter, the past experiences that triggered off this resentment occurred in childhood or early teenage years, and the writer may not be consciously aware of them any longer. Smouldering in the subconscious mind, this unresolved hostility forms the roots of his or her present grudge-bearing nature, and will continue to do so, until professional help is sought.

This unfortunate characteristic has the potential to completely ruin the love life of even the most sexually compatible of partners. In an intimate relationship, if such people are hurt by nasty words or actions during the heat of a fierce argument, they are capable of sulking for an extended period of time, and bitter resentment will be felt towards the 'aggressor'. In such instances lovemaking will obviously be avoided at all costs, and this state of affairs will continue for an unknown duration. Even when this mood eventually abates, there is a good chance they will mention the matter again in the future in order to once more punish a partner.

Anyone living with such an individual will need tremendous self-restraint if there is to be any chance of a satisfying sex life. Disagreements will have to be resolved with intelligent discussion, rather than intense emotion, to avoid any possibility of an exchange of harsh words. Also, this person has a strong desire to control, and will want to make all the decisions in the relationship, unless mutual agreement is first reached as to the division of responsibilities.

THE OPEN-MOUTHED OVAL

The capital or small letters 'a' and 'o' with a wide gap at the top:

Sigmund Freud would have cheerfully classified this particular specimen of *Homo sapiens* as being 'orally fixated'. Indeed, when not engaged in conversation, it is very possible that the 'oral cavity' will be soothed by a cigar, cigarette, piece of chewing gum and perhaps just the tops of the fingernails. Alternatively, you may be dealing with a compulsive nibbler who eats between meals and then complains about weight problems!

The oral character of such people can easily be distinguished by their strong desire to talk, and the great pleasure they derive from speech. You will never have to push them to give you their opinions, because they will do so whether you like it or not.

If you are planning to share a life with a person like this, resign yourself to astronomic telephone accounts and be prepared to fight for your turn to speak, as these types are highly egocentric in their manner of communication. They tend to monopolize the conversation and have trouble listening, as even when they do give others time to speak, they are still wrapped up in their own thoughts or busy thinking about their replies, and so they fail to accurately tune in to what is being said.

Such individuals are frequently compulsive talkers, and unless they know someone very well, they are likely to feel very uncomfortable during moments of silence, which they will try to fill with incessant chatter.

Many people with this characteristic love to talk about themselves, generally in a favourable light. They find it easy to take centre stage, and are quite at ease with their somewhat exhibitionist behaviour, which is motivated by their desire to gain attention, admiration and affection. Usually this craving to express themselves verbally goes with a marked degree of verbal intelligence and fluency.

The self-image of these people fluctuates considerably according to their moods. When they are in a phase of well-being and excitement, they have an exaggeratedly positive view of their personality and potential; at other times, when they are aware of the darker and more sombre aspects of reality, they are capable of negating the existence of any genuinely positive qualities in their personality, becoming overwhelmed by feelings of helplessness, inadequacy and pessimism.

Another component of this oral character is the recurrent feeling of inner emptiness and loneliness even when involved in a love relationship, though this may not be evident from the outward manner. Often the oral type is reluctant to accept the reality and the necessity of struggle in life.

Although oral characters can become highly irritable, and are capable of much sound and fury, the strong feeling of genuine uncontrolled anger is a very rare phenomenon in such people. Indeed the old cliché, 'their bark is far worse than their bite', is an apt description of the way in which they express hostile feelings.

The development of this personality can always be traced back to feelings of emotional deprivation during childhood. Individuals with this trait invariably experienced a sense of hopelessness because they felt rejected or abandoned by a mother-figure, who for some reason failed to satisfy their needs and longing for care and affection.

Involvement with a full-time career, or maybe a severely handicapped child, may have prevented the mother from devoting sufficient time to the needs of her offspring, or alternatively, numerous other possible causes may have been responsible, ranging from simple neglect, or separation due to schooling or divorce proceedings, to unavoidable life events such as early death. Whatever the reason, the child was forced to become prematurely emotionally independent, creating simultaneously this deep-seated insecurity in the personality.

In relationships these people have a tendency to be the clinging, emotionally dependent, narcissistic type, being highly demanding in the sense that they will constantly expect abundant sympathy, understanding and demonstrative displays of love and affection. If they do not receive these, they are very prone to feelings of rejection.

They are overly sensitive to any coldness in their partners, though they may well fail to notice those times when they themselves might be lacking in warmth. It almost seems as if they look upon a mate as someone who is there to supply their narcissistic needs in life, much in the same way as a young infant regards a mother. When an oral type deeply loves someone therefore, this unfortunately is usually experienced by their partner as a demand for love instead.

In relationships, their tendency to talk too much prevents them from reaching a deeper level of connectedness with their mates, as it often forces communication to remain at the more superficial level of the intellect, and blocks the opportunity for expressing and receiving those heartfelt feelings which occur at deeper levels of interaction. Compulsive talkers invariably suffer from an excess of nervous energy, and chattering is the body's way of releasing some of it. They would however, clearly do themselves and others a great service if they chose to discharge this tension via sport or some other physical activity.

People with this graphological characteristic are often strongly attracted to the oral components of the lovemaking ritual, though in order to be sure that the following description of women and men in this category applies, you will need to check other areas of this book for other traits (for instance signs of sexual repression or sadistic inclinations) which could disrupt or block the personality tendencies described below.

Women with this trait will adore prolonging foreplay, to indulge in an abundance of warm, loving embraces, and they will be able to wallow for ages amidst the sensual pleasure of slow, deeply felt, sensuous kissing. They find sweet, sexy, love talk highly arousing, and so any lover who takes the time to include plenty of this erotic chatter in the repertoire will find his efforts well rewarded. Women with this characteristic are also generally not averse to giving and receiving oral sex, but are unlikely to be as obsessed with this area as their male counterparts tend to be.

Men with this sign in their writing also love to spend a great deal of time with passionate hugging and deep, erotic, lip kissing, and many such individuals can really get carried away when it comes to kissing and sucking the breasts of their lovers. Indeed this may well reflect a temporary regression to the infant stage of their development when such needs were denied them due to premature weaning.

The high point of the whole lovemaking ceremony however, for males in this category, is without any doubt oral sex. These individuals are likely to gain great pleasure if their mates perform oral sex on them, but what they will enjoy even more, is when they can escape all the fears and anxieties of existence by losing themselves in the warm, exciting, sensual pleasure of deeply kissing their woman's 'yoni' (the beautiful, poetical Sanskrit word for vagina).

These people are likely to fully understand from their own experience, and will therefore heartily agree with Eastern erotic mythology when it compares cunnilingus, or orally loving a woman, to the relationship between the bee and the lotus flower: due to the exciting provocation of the bee's activities deep in the lotus, the flower eventually climaxes, secreting nectar-like substances of great beauty and nourishing sweetness. In the Hindu way of thinking, the fluids that a woman secretes during arousal, and especially during orgasm, are considered nectar of the goddess. These fluids, imbibed orally, are considered highly beneficial to male well-being. The Chinese Taoist masters of eroticism also enthusiastically agree with this point. It will obviously come as no surprise to learn, therefore, that in many males with this graphological characteristic '69' is a highly favoured position in the sexual repertoire.

THE WHIP

Capital or small letters with a final line that rises
noticeably higher and curves or 'whips' to the right:

W H V N

As its name suggests, this particular graphological stroke is
not a particularly pleasant one in its effect on intimate
relationships.

People who have this sign in their writing are invariably
difficult to live with, as they have a highly competitive,
aggressive nature, and are generally on some sort of power
trip. No matter how charming they may be at the start of
a new relationship, once they feel someone is emotionally
attached to them, they will show their true colours by
manipulating themselves into a position of total control,
where they can indulge their pleasure in handing out
commands and instructions.

If they are with a partner who tries to control them in
any way, they will find this intolerable, as taking orders is
very stressful for them. They are capable of being unusually
obstinate, and in arguments can be very rigid and
uncompromising, so don't expect them to give in and
apologize first. On the positive side, they will undoubtedly
stand by their mates in the face of danger, and can be relied
upon to cope successfully in situations that call for the
survival instinct.

A woman with this characteristic will never succumb to
the sexual advances of her partner, no matter how
persuasive, unless she is equally in the mood for such
intimacies. Assuming she has no specific problems in her

attitude to sex, she is likely to be quite explicit in terms of exactly how she wishes foreplay and intercourse to be conducted. If her writing also shows a vivid sexual fantasy, then you can be sure she will enjoy introducing some erotic games into the repertoire; these will undoubtedly include some borderline 'power-oriented' games where one partner plays a very submissive role.

Indeed, women with the sign of 'The Whip' in their writing can be a real 'turn on' in the bedroom, but only as long as they are with someone for whom they have a high regard.

If such a woman lacks respect for her man, sexual activity will be kept to a bare minimum, and instead her energy will be channelled totally into her career (many women with this graphological sign are very successful high achievers). If she has no such outlet, she will simply make her partner's life a misery with endless complaining and criticism.

A man with this trait is bound to be sexually very demanding, and will expect satisfaction when and where he considers it appropriate. Unless he has other signs in his writing, revealing traits that balance his rather harsh nature, his manner of lovemaking is unlikely to be particularly satisfying; these types tend to avoid the romantic approach to sex and lack the sort of softness and sensitivity that many women yearn for. Instead, they are likely to prefer a wilder more lustful style, that expresses virility rather than love. For many of them sex is simply an arena where they can demonstrate their manliness and skills, in expectation of 'applause' from a partner in the form of a real (or feigned) expression of sheer pleasure. Indeed, if such a man does not manage to trigger off an orgasm in his mate, he will feel he has failed, as he cannot conceive that it is possible for his partner sometimes equally to enjoy intercourse without the physical orgasm, via the mutual expression of deeply felt love.

People with this writing sign always expect others to conform closely to their own standards of behaviour, and can be very judgmental and critical of anyone who does not harmonize with their rigidly defined views of how one should live. During arguments, past errors will be recalled, together with other criticisms, as evidence of a mate's imperfections, and satisfaction will be derived from pointing out weaknesses in an insensitive and disparaging manner. They can also be very skilful in subtly undermining their partner's confidence, which will badly damage their self-esteem, and this is precisely the motive (albeit subconscious) behind the fault-finder's actions. Such people are in fact extremely self-critical (even if this is not evident), and seek to relieve the pain of this negative self-assessment by diminishing other people's worth, so that in comparison they seem to be better. This unpleasant behaviour is the result of a futile attempt to escape from a deeply rooted lack of self-respect, that probably developed in childhood amidst an atmosphere of excessive judgment and criticism.

A man with this trait may well have a tendency to criticize his partner's physical appearance whilst pointing out the attractive physiques of other women, or alternatively, he may nag about domestic inefficiency, social slip-ups, or the quality of his sex life.

A woman with this trait (unless she is exceptionally happy with her partner) will tend to attack her man's career, perhaps complaining about his insufficient earnings, or unsociable working hours. In addition, friends, style of lovemaking, and perhaps his general attitude towards women and sex, could also be targets for criticism, and there will inevitably be complaints about home life, and existence in general.

To sum up, a lot of work will be needed in order to create a successful relationship and sex life with any individual who has 'The Whip' in his or her writing. To have any hope of succeeding in this endeavour, a prospective partner will not only need to have an evolved awareness of human nature, but also a strong and compassionate personality.

THE DEVIOUS LOOP

Capital or small letters with a double or treble loop:

advance precisely look flag

Great care must be taken when interpreting this particular graphological trait. In handwriting with no obvious sign of aggression, or excessive drive for money or power (check the rest of the graphological alphabet to determine this), the expression of this characteristic will probably be entirely benign. If, however, there are clear indications of hostility, financial greed, or strong cravings to be in a position of control over others, this same writing sign is likely to have distinctly negative connotations.

In the former case, these 'tangled loops' could easily feature in the handwriting of an essentially benevolent, good-hearted soul, who may have a tendency to exaggerate or tell harmless tall stories and white lies. There are various possible reasons for such behaviour; the inclination to tell white lies, for instance, is usually motivated by a desire to boost another person's self-esteem, or lift their spirits, by hiding some unpleasant truth that would otherwise dampen enthusiasm.

These types invariably have self-condemnatory
tendencies and a poor sense of their own worth; even if
highly competent and successful, they will nevertheless
imagine weaknesses in themselves, and greatly undervalue
their qualities and achievements. It is also probable that
they still live with regrets about various golden
opportunities they may have missed in life. This frustration
and deep sense of unfulfilment unfortunately predisposes
them towards over-indulgence in self-destructive habits
such as smoking and drinking, and if they do not eventually
find some other more positive means of release, they may
seriously injure their health.

Wishing to hide their feelings of inadequacy, for fear of
being rejected or negatively judged, they may have
developed the habit of embroidering or overstating the
truth, in order to please others, and create an impression of
strength and self-assurance. This behaviour pattern is often
quite unnecessary, as they may in reality be highly capable,
but simply have failed to accept this truth.

In relationships, their self-protective attitude and
insecure self-image will make them frightened of rejection,
and they are likely to cloak their innermost thoughts and
feelings in a veil of secrecy, until a powerful feeling of
mutual love and trust builds up between them and a
partner.

Their skill in stretching the truth will certainly come in
handy if they are in a relationship with a domineering,
fault-finding type as, when the 'rules of the establishment'
are broken, you can be sure they will concoct some brilliant
excuse or explanation for their conduct in order to escape
punishment. If they feel threatened in any way, their
behaviour immediately becomes highly guarded and
secretive. In an unhappy and stormy relationship, these and
other evasion tactics will become a way of life, being the

key weapon in this person's armoury of self-defence.

Such behaviour usually has its source in a childhood ruled by an atmosphere of repression, harsh judgment and sometimes excessive pressure to achieve. This may have stemmed from the family home, and/or the school environment. Having a low tolerance threshold for such pressures, such people discover at an early age that they can reduce the amount they suffer by adapting the truth and inventing ingenious excuses. This self-reinforcing strategy is highly successful in extricating them from situations that would otherwise lead to their being blamed and chastised. Thus, this *modus operandi* becomes an intrinsic structure in their personality.

The dark side of this behaviour pattern inevitably emerges when this writing characteristic is seen in combination with an intense desire for money or power (revealed in writing by various traits, such as very long, balloon-shaped lower stems, extremely large or highly flamboyant capitals, blunt 'club-shaped' endings, triangular shaped stems etc.). In such cases, the following description will be applicable.

If you find honesty an attractive feature of human nature, you will be very disappointed with this character. To say this person can 'stretch the truth' would be a gross underestimation of a limitless capacity to blatantly lie. Such individuals will not hesitate to evade, disguise, distort or smother the truth in pursuit of their ambitions – usually at other people's expense. Premeditated, carefully calculated lies form an essential part of their daily survival strategy and their sly, cunning, crafty nature makes it incredibly easy for them to hide their true motives and intentions in order to deceive, manipulate and cheat others to satisfy their own needs and desires.

For the sake of personal gain, they are able to adapt

themselves to others so adroitly that they can appear incredibly interested in and fascinated by those they do not even slightly care about.

If you are contemplating a first date with such a person, remember that the face you see in public bears little resemblance to his or her true inner nature. In conversation, such people will masterfully cover up the undesirable aspects of their personality, substituting for these pure make-believe, designed to impress and attract. Anything you are told about their previous relationships and sex life should definitely be taken with 'a pinch of salt'. If you are a sucker for flattery, and they happen to notice this, you can be quite certain the knowledge will be used to their advantage. A wonderful bouquet of beautifully chosen praise will be delivered, in an attempt to manipulate you into succumbing to their desires.

Their skill in hiding the truth should turn out to be an undeniable asset to them if they also happen to have an unfaithful streak in their personality. This devious, underhand, master of falsehood and disguise is bound to arrange things so that no one else has even an inkling of suspicion that anything is going on.

Underneath whatever act such a person has contrived exists an anxious, frightened, tense character, with a very low sense of self-worth. These individuals live under the constant stress of being found out, their life of deceit is a major source of hardship for them, and the continual suppression of their real thoughts and feelings at times becomes unbearably exhausting. In their desperate efforts to relieve the intense frustration and pressure of their existence, these types frequently seek support from damaging habits such as excessive drinking or smoking, though if questioned about this, there is a good chance they will insist that they do so only in moderation.

This whole reaction to existence is invariably a product of early emotional and material deprivation. Childhood, for these individuals, is filled with unpleasant memories of pain and struggle. This unfortunate background has conditioned a psyche driven by fear, and shaped a mind dominated solely by thoughts of personal survival, no matter what the cost. Sacrificing integrity to get what one wants from life is for this individual a small price to pay. It is highly improbable that such a person's conscience will be even slightly troubled by this dishonest manner of living.

If you are considering a serious relationship with this individual, you would clearly be well advised to first thoroughly check out anything you are told. If you can somehow manage to arrange a meeting with at least one previous long-term partner, this would undoubtedly be the most reliable way to discover the truth about such a person's real nature, before you get too heavily involved.

Finally, it needs to be stated that occasionally one will come across someone with this graphological sign who exhibits no dishonest behaviour whatsoever. Such examples however, are extremely rare, and will only be found in individuals who have chosen to evolve their consciousness through meditative practice, or some other mind-expanding pursuit. In such instances, though dishonest tendencies may still exist, and appear in the writing, they no longer govern this person's actions, as the strength of his or her self-awareness has neutralized any such influences.

THE SPIRAL

Capital or small letters containing a spiral shape:

A E f a d e g y

This graphological feature is a gesture of concealment. When it is seen in someone's writing, one can be sure that he or she is carefully hiding from others certain troubling thoughts and feelings which are too embarrassing, or shaming, to disclose.

In a woman, there may be a hidden fear of sex, or an excessive concern with some aspect of her physical appearance.

Men with this sign in their writing often seem to have a penis fixation, and may find it difficult to stop thinking about this organ. There is likely to be anxiety about its size, fears about its performance, and there could also be subconscious guilt feelings attached to the act of self-stimulation.

People with spirals in their writing are particularly prone to becoming obsessed with worrying thoughts or problems to which they attach an exaggerated level of importance, and this tendency stems from a general underlying current of emotional insecurity, dating back to childhood. In relationships, this has made them fear rivalry, and though they may conceal the fact, jealous feelings grip them from time to time.

Often, these people have experienced a great deal of suffering during their early formative years, as a result of either emotional or material deprivation, and this may have made them over-anxious about money matters. Anyone in a relationship with such a person will probably have to work very hard to persuade him or her to accept the idea of spending money on any items that are considered unessential. Usually such individuals are natural survivors with great strength of spirit, so when the going gets tough in life they can generally manage to keep things together.

A person who makes a spiral formation on the lower stems of letters, for example, on the stems of the 'y' or 'g' is liable to be very materialistic and greedy, and in addition, there will be a massive amount of secrecy with regard to private life and sexual behaviour.

Such people are almost always very self-centred and egocentric in relationship, and desiring to draw attention to themselves can display a distinct streak of vanity, but on social occasions, if they set their sights on a potential partner, they can be unusually charming, attractive and sexually seductive in order to 'hook' their new catch.

People with this sign in their lower stems have very unusual sexual tastes and are bound to get a real kick out of weird lovers and kinky sex games. They will be bored by what most people regard as normal sex, and will quickly tire of any mate who does not have an interest in way out erotic practices.

If there are many examples in the writing of letters containing a spiral-shaped formation, this person will also be a narcissist. If this is the case, the description given in 'Everybody, Look at Me! Am I Wonderful?' page 227, will also apply.

For further information on the sexual behaviour patterns and other aspects of personality connected with this graphological characteristic, see 'The Kinky Lover', page 261.

THE KNOT

Capital or small letters that are 'tied' with a knot:

A, for R the H sit

Persistence is without doubt a central characteristic of people who form knots in their writing. Indeed the motto 'never give up' would be an apt description of their general attitude to existence. When the knot is made with a noticeably large loop this also indicates great pride in one's own and one's family's achievements. Such a person will certainly be unusually proud of any mate who achieves well, or who is talented or artistic.

When a goal is set, neither adversity nor failure will discourage such people for long. So when the going gets tough in a close relationship, they will do their best to work things out, rather than just abandon ship. Unfortunately though, some people with this writing sign may display an exaggerated version of this characteristic, and even when it is quite obvious that a relationship is incompatible, unworkable and thus doomed to failure, they nevertheless find it impossible to let go. Instead they persistently and anxiously hold on to something that has no future because they are too afraid to release the past and get on with their life anew.

If people make knots on their lower stems, for example on the 'g' or 'y', this indicates an exaggerated form of persistence that is manifested as compulsive or obsessive behaviour patterns. Such people are usually very vain, overconcerned with outer appearances and they often have a streak of snobbishness in their personality. Capable of being very petty-minded and fussy about insignificant matters, they can at times display tremendous obstinacy when their mind is set.

This unusual formation of stem also points to an underlying eccentricity in sexual tastes, though a mate is unlikely to be aware of this early on in a relationship, as these types have to build up a fair amount of trust in someone before this side of their nature expresses itself.

If it is possible to do so, it would obviously be a good idea to find out more about this person's sexual preferences before you become too involved, as otherwise there is clearly a risk that at some later stage you may discover an aspect of sexual behaviour you find unacceptable.

THE JAGGED TOWER

Begins with a sharply angled peak rising noticeably above the rest of the letter:

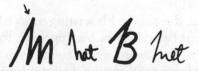

Without doubt, this character is on some kind of power trip, which has fuelled him or her with abundant motivation to achieve a position of prominence in life.

Such people want others to see them as impressive, dynamic and commanding personalities, probably in order to regain a loss of power experienced during childhood, as a result of being dominated by an overbearing parent-figure.

This particular combination of attributes has, unfortunately, some negative side-effects. In an intimate relationship, discontentment is a certainty if such a person is not able to be in a position of control over a respectful and admiring partner.

People with this graphological characteristic are bound to be somewhat domineering and judgmental, and may well gain satisfaction from insensitively highlighting and criticizing their partners' weaknesses in order to embarrass and humiliate them into losing their self-confidence. They do this in an attempt to reinforce their own sense of superiority, which, in reality, is simply a facade that conceals low self-esteem.

In lovemaking, a woman with this trait will never passively oblige her partner's advances unless she herself is very much in the mood for sex, and you can be fairly certain that she will let her lover know, in no uncertain terms, if his love play is not up to standard. Indeed, when such a woman is with someone who regularly fails to please her sexually, she may well launch a vicious attack on his virility that will remain firmly imprinted in his memory for the rest of his life.

A man with this sign in his writing tends to adopt a very macho style of behaviour in his approach to lovemaking, and is often far more concerned with creating an impression of powerful virility than with tuning into the subtle, sensual needs of his mate.

Generally egocentric and lacking in sensitivity, such men are rarely considered good lovers, though in the early stages of a new relationship certain women may find this macho image a real, but very temporary, turn-on.

If a man in this category has a high sex drive, even if his partner is not in the mood, he is nevertheless likely to do his utmost to coerce her into sexual activity. If this graphological sign is seen in writing which is very muddy and dirty in appearance (denoting very animal-like sensual passion), there is a very strong chance that such an individual will sometimes use physical force upon his lover.

THE FISH-HOOK

Writing with many examples of little hook formations appearing on capital or small letters:

Natural survivors with a fighting instinct and considerable strength of spirit, people with this graphological characteristic are always on the alert, and will cope better than most with the obstacles and hardships encountered on their journey through life. Though their aggressive, competitive nature may serve them well in many areas, in relationships it will undoubtedly make them difficult to live with.

Always ready to argue, they will rarely be the one to give in and apologize first, and when their minds are made up, they are unlikely ever to consider compromise as an alternative. In addition, when their temper shows itself, they can become very unpleasant, judgmental and fault-finding. On the positive side however, they have a strong survival instinct, and would fearlessly protect loved ones in the face of danger.

Having a somewhat overactive sympathetic nervous system or 'fight/flight' response, they are inclined to become very stressed and irritable at times, and as a reaction to this they could be drawn to self-destructive habits, such as overeating, drinking or smoking.

When this graphological characteristic appears there is a strong likelihood that the person concerned experienced much emotional and/or material deprivation during the formative years, and if so, the consequential deep-rooted feelings of insecurity are likely to have produced a highly acquisitive streak in the personality.

Emotionally such people are liable to be very demanding and will probably be quite possessive. If their sex drive is strong, they will invariably expect satisfaction on a regular basis, and if refused will become very irritable and unfriendly as they will interpret such rebuttals as a sign of personal rejection. Many men with this graphological characteristic tend to need sex very regularly, to release the build-up of pressure stemming from their over-adrenalized, stressful natures.

THE SHARK'S TOOTH

**Capital or small letters that contain
a 'shark's tooth' shape:**

Maytime, here we are now!

This person's strong fighting spirit and fox-like survival instinct will overcome any hindrances met along the path to achieving life's goals. Possessing a cunning, scheming nature, such people are very crafty in their manner of dealing with others, and are quite capable when necessary of skilfully hiding the truth in order to escape from a pressured situation or difficult dilemma; if all else fails, they can also tell blatant lies in a thoroughly convincing manner.

Life will probably not be easy in a relationship with these individuals, as whenever their temper shows itself, they become judgmental and fault-finding, and will sharply and ruthlessly criticize the most vulnerable areas of a partner's ego. In addition, they are likely to have double standards, and can be expected to be quite hypocritical and unjust at times.

Because they find it easy to hide the truth, one obviously cannot guarantee their fidelity in a monogamous relationship. If their sex life is unsatisfactory, and an opportunity presents itself, then they are quite capable, if they choose, of carefully concealing any amorous encounters they may have on the side, and their mates are unlikely to have even an inkling of what is going on.

THE TICK

**Capital or small letters with a very short,
rigid diagonal line attached, that starts from
well above the baseline:**

$$Hm \; Kp \; Mw \; \partial n$$

This graphological sign reveals someone who is at times very impatient, short-tempered and irritable. Fortunately however, any such outbursts are generally very short-lived as this person can usually re-establish emotional equilibrium quite rapidly.

Such people are extremely critical of themselves and those around them, and in an intimate relationship this will mean that they will sometimes be very harsh and judgmental towards a partner. Enjoying possessions, they are likely to be acquisitive and could well derive great satisfaction from hobbies that involve building up some sort of collection.

Relationships with such individuals are bound to be a bit of a roller-coaster at times, as their moods fluctuate rapidly, so you will never really know quite where you stand with them. Depending on other attributes in their personality, their unpredictable sexual nature could alter very dramatically, ranging from warm and passionate at times, all the way to the other end of the spectrum where they can suddenly become cold and uninterested.

Such a changeable temperament was probably moulded by an atmosphere of great parental conflict during childhood years. Unexpressed anger towards their parents, that was undoubtedly stored in these people's subconscious, is now periodically released via the previously mentioned angry outbursts. If you are living with such an individual, take note of this explanation and try not to take any unpleasantness too much to heart, as the irritability clearly lies within the person, and is therefore not your fault or responsibility.

THE SMUDGE

Capital or small letters that are ink-filled or 'smudgy' in appearance:

George and Cathy have come

The exciting joys of Security are here.

The primal instinctive need to satisfy the sensual appetites is especially active in this particular individual. Extra-sensitive tastebuds and a developed sense of touch have probably led to a very passionate appetite for food and sex, so there may well be a need to guard against over-indulgence. This person should certainly steer well clear of any lovers who have an abstinent or ascetic nature.

For detailed information on the sexual behaviour and other aspects of personality connected with this graphological characteristic, see 'The Sensual Lover', page 271.

THE NEEDLE

Capital or small letters which contain a sharp needle point:

Writing with many examples of letters containing a sharp needle point discloses a nature capable of great fluctuation with regard to the personality characteristics of cruelty and kindness. Although some individuals with this graphological characteristic may turn out to have extremely pleasant personalities (depending on other factors in the writing), very often when one comes across this trait it betrays a human being who is likely to create a great deal of unhappiness in a relationship. Such people often have fast minds and a speedy manner of living, and any mate who keeps them waiting, or is long-winded or slow in thinking, will be treated disrespectfully and may be on the receiving end of downright rudeness. They will often be sharp-tongued and sarcastic when irritable or angry, and if a partner falls far below their expectations they will feel very bitter, and could well become openly contemptuous and derisive. If a mate has a powerful personality that will not allow for such negative behaviour, they will instead release their pent-up feelings via silent glances that are scornful or mocking.

Frequently lacking in sensuality and warmth, such individuals find it difficult to establish close physical or emotional connectedness with others, and consequently their mode of lovemaking is unlikely to be particularly stimulating or exciting. Even if they make a great effort to satisfy a mate, the result will probably be disappointing. They find it difficult to express genuine passion, and are usually so out of contact with their own and their partners' feelings that they become incapable of touching or caressing in a loving, sensitive and sensual manner. Their mates may well find themselves feeling sexually dissatisfied and possibly even lonely and unloved.

THE BLUNT CLUB

Capital or small letters with a blunt, 'club-shaped' part:

A E G got and at are

Submissiveness and consideration are virtues that are almost unknown to this person; a compulsive drive to control people is combined with an excessively aggressive temperament that will rapidly intimidate weaker beings into submission. Capable of turning into a one-man army when intent on succeeding in objectives, if thwarted such an individual can become extremely angry and belligerent.

These people have a tough, warrior-like spirit, and will pursue their objectives with much intensity and little hesitation. Their highly competitive, ambitious nature will not allow them to stop, until they succeed. In a relationship, they will rule the home environment with an iron hand. When angry, they will point out faults in a partner's personality, in a blunt, insensitive manner, in order to destroy self-confidence and humiliate. Such people need to feel superior to others to compensate for underlying feelings of inadequacy developed during their early years.

It is likely that this individual's personality is the product of a childhood controlled by a domineering parent-figure. As a child, such a person may have been subjected to physical punishment, which created frustrated, angry feelings.

When such people lose their temper, they are quite capable of expressing their anger physically. Women with this handwriting characteristic however, are unlikely to exhibit nearly as much violent behaviour as men with the same sign. This is partly due to differently conditioned attitudes towards violence in males and females, but the main influencing factor is that males have far greater amounts of testosterone in their bodies, and this hormone is directly connected with both sexual and aggressive behaviour. (A more complete discussion of this matter can be found in 'Are You In Danger?' page 216.)

People with this graphological sign (especially men) may choose to settle an argument with their fists if they lack emotional self-control and feel they are losing ground in a confrontation. Indeed, should some unfortunate soul dare openly to express hostility towards this person, they will incur such wrath that self-exile to Siberia might not seem like such a bad alternative.

If you are contemplating an intimate relationship with this person, think twice, unless you happen to be a master of martial arts or a lion tamer.

The different hormonal balance in men and women explains the following significant contrast between them, in terms of violent behaviour as well as sexual urges.

If a man's writing produces a blunt club-shaped formation on the lower stems of letters, for example on the stems of the letter 'g' or 'y', you can be 100 per cent certain that the primitive animal-like side of his nature lies very close to the surface. Consequently, he will have tremendous difficulty in controlling his basic, instinctual urges, as the more civilized and evolved portion of his consciousness is often completely overwhelmed by intense sexual cravings and uncontrollable aggressive impulses.

An enormous amount of anger is being repressed, and the immense pressure of this internally held emotion has built up to a dangerously high level. Unless he finds some sort of harmless physical release for this pent-up energy, there is a good chance that this contained anger will be expressed in a very cruel, violent and even sadistic fashion. Possessing the ability to easily con or manipulate others, and bluff an appearance of good will and friendliness, this individual will be able to effectively conceal this severely disturbed, hostile nature, and his warped behaviour will usually be carefully and skilfully hidden from all except those unfortunate enough to be on the receiving end.

This person undoubtedly experiences very powerful sexual urges, and in lovemaking his harsh, self-obsessed nature is likely to make him very egocentric, inconsiderate, and highly inattentive of his partner's needs and feelings. Lacking any genuine kindness or sensitivity, he will easily become frustrated and angry if deprived of sufficient sexual release. Such men also have a lowered resistance to sexual excesses and perversions. They could well be devotees of heavy-duty sadomasochistic routines, indulging in excessively violent forms of sexual domination such as 'mock rape' or dangerous bondage 'games'. In certain rare cases, a man with this graphological characteristic may be living with a women who completely controls him, and he will therefore find himself unable to openly express his hostile nature, and sadistic, power-oriented sexual desires. This can have seriously negative side-effects, as the internal pressure could build up to the point where some other unfortunate person will become the victim of his violent impulses.

The roots of this potentially malevolent psyche can inevitably be traced back to an extremely sick parental relationship, which produced feelings of deep rage that remain hidden and festering to this day. As a child, this person may well have experienced strong self-destructive impulses, or else he may have harboured a conscious or possibly unconscious desire to physically injure one or both of his parents as a result of the mistreatment he has received. This perhaps explains his current wish to hurt other people. His victims have become scapegoats for this repressed hatred of a parent.

Women with this trait have a strong libido, but are far more in control of their sexual urges than their male counterparts. They will certainly not be sexually passive, and will never succumb to the desires of their partner unless they, too, are in the mood for sex. Sexually very explicit, these women are usually quite happy to tell their mates exactly what they want them to do in bed, and their desires may turn out to be quite unusual. Such women invariably enjoy dominating their men, as they need and want to be in full charge of the relationship. During sexual intercourse, therefore, they may well favour those positions which place them in the 'masculine' or dominant role. This perhaps explains why women with this characteristic are often attracted to men with distinctly soft, feminine qualities who are prepared to take the subordinate position in the relationship. If such a woman's partner strives instead to dominate her, she will become very angry, and there is bound to be a great deal of conflict. Under these circumstances, she may well become physically violent towards her mate.

Some women in this category have very ambivalent feelings towards the male population in general, and this can make them extremely moody in a relationship. Sometimes one comes across women with this trait who dislike men intensely, and who will often avoid sex altogether, preferring to sublimate their potentially powerful appetites in this area via their career and/or family. In such instances, a partner is likely to have a miserable existence, and may well be on the receiving end of considerable psychological and even physical hostility.

It hardly needs stating that, if you see this graphological sign in someone's writing, you would do well to avoid them like the plague! However, you should note that blunt, club-shaped formations are sometimes seen in the handwriting of individuals who quite obviously have a developed intellect and good emotional self-control. In such instances, it is possible that many of the negative behaviour patterns described above will rarely express themselves in the personality. Instead such individuals often succeed in channelling their extremely aggressive inclinations in a socially acceptable manner.

For example, Ernest Hemingway sometimes formed club-shaped lower stems. He chose however, to release his aggressive impulses on paper, with violent stories of war and in addition he killed animals during hunting excursions, which at the time was an entirely acceptable form of behaviour.

It is interesting to note however, that his emotional and intellectual self-control sometimes lapsed, and on such occasions he would often become involved in very violent bar-room brawls. Towards the end of his life though, it seems that his aggressive tendencies turned inwards on himself, culminating in a final act of ultimate self-destruction – suicide.

THE SHARP KNIFE

> **Capital or small letters containing a razor sharp, 'knife-like' formation:**
>
> $\mathcal{D} \mathcal{C} \dot{\mathcal{S}} \mathcal{S} \mathcal{g} \mathcal{h} \mathcal{f} \mathcal{y}$

Those in search of a peaceful, loving mate should definitely give this one a miss, as this person is filled with tremendous anger and goes through life harbouring grudges towards others.

Such people, if they feel someone has purposefully hurt them, will do their utmost to pay them back, for they have an exceptionally vengeful nature and will wish harm on anyone they consider an enemy. This intense hostility undoubtedly betrays a deeply ingrained hatred towards a parent-figure that is rooted in a childhood filled with bitterness and conflict. The pain such people felt as children has remained with them to the present day and reveals itself in their desire to inflict suffering on others.

In a relationship, this rather unsavoury personality will be very unpleasant to live with, highly critical, and at times downright nasty, with a domineering, harsh manner that will sometimes destroy a partner's confidence and squash his or her individuality.

If such people make a razor-sharp, knife-like formation on the lower stems of letters, for example on the stems of the letter 'g' or 'y', in addition to all the above they will also feel great frustration and anger in the area of sex. Their approach to lovemaking will invariably lack sensitivity and softness, and they will generally be unconcerned about a partner's needs and feelings. Some people with this trait may gain enjoyment from sex games which are somewhat sadistic or cruel.

If the writing has a dirty, muddy-looking appearance in combination with these lower stem knives, then watch out! This graphological mixture is frequently found in the writing of criminals, and sex offenders in particular, though if someone with these writing signs also has a good intellect and at least a fair sense of right and wrong, it is highly unlikely that such extreme behaviour will be manifested in the personality.

Indeed, as with all negative characteristics found in writing, if such people have chosen to evolve their self-awareness, then they may well have also succeeded in sublimating the darker aspects of their nature in a manner that causes no one any harm.

3. Capital Letters

HANDWRITING FEATURES THAT CAN APPEAR ON ANY CAPITAL LETTER

At least three and a half times the height of the central zone:

Robert Smith *Dear*

This lively attention seeker knows how to switch on the charisma, whilst hiding behind a convincing facade of showmanship, so if you have just started dating him or her, remember that what you see now is unlikely to be what you get later.

People like this have a sense of pride that borders on vanity, and they require frequent praise and reassurance to maintain confidence in their sexuality. In a relationship, therefore, to have any chance of finding erotic satisfaction, they need to be with someone who considers them highly desirable and a wonderful lover.

If they feel a partner does not really fancy them any longer, this could devastate their sexual self-esteem, and they could well be tempted to search for someone else who can re-inflate their drooping libido.

Large and showy:

WBDHEF

This individual's strong social presence combines with abundant charisma and a natural sense of showmanship and poise to project a highly credible and impressive image. In reality, though, this is a veneer which hides tremendous feelings of inadequacy and insecurity that probably originated in a childhood in which he or she felt either underprivileged or rejected in some way.

Burning hunger for constant approval and respect becomes the controlling force in such people's lives, making them extremely difficult to live with in a long-term relationship. They are constantly anxious, terrified of failure, and their self-obsession and egocentricity sometimes dominates so much of their awareness that they can completely lose sight of a partner's feelings and needs. Their exaggerated desire for status and public recognition makes them critical of any mate who is not impressive enough to support their social image.

These types are bound to be over-concerned with their physical appearance; a man with this trait is often highly critical of his own body, and is always very dissatisfied with the size of his penis (unless he is lucky enough to be extremely well endowed).

A woman with this writing characteristic will tend to be critical of her breasts, buttocks, or stomach, if not of her whole figure.

To enjoy lovemaking, it is crucial for a man with this characteristic to have a partner who finds his sexual allure irresistible. Nothing less can hope to soothe his underlying fears with regard to his sexual attractiveness or performance in bed. Even then, such men are still not often pleased with themselves, as their self-expectations in this area are likely to be so high that unless they happen to be genuine sexual athletes they will inevitably be very self-critical. In such intimate situations, if they are criticized or undervalued in any way, their sexual ego will be irreparably bruised. They will certainly not hesitate to look elsewhere for satisfaction if they think their mate is no longer turned on by them, as they are not capable of tolerating this type of blow to their libido.

Finally, anyone dating such a person should remember that the old cliché 'appearances can be deceptive' without any doubt applies to this character. Such people's fear of not being accepted for who they really are, makes it virtually impossible for them to reveal their true selves until they have built up substantial trust in someone, over a long period of time.

Extended horizontally:

Charlie Even Regards Love

Who cares about modesty? This person struts through life confident of being among the world's sexiest people, and subscribing firmly to the idea that if you've got it, you should flaunt it.

Feeling good with themselves, as they generally do, makes such people fun to have around: they can start a buzz, or spark a day, a party, a person into life, and they honestly believe that they can take the fun straight into bed.

They certainly give the impression of being really hot stuff between the sheets, or beneath the duvet – but are they really? You had better check out their lower extensions before you decide (in other words, look up the meaning of their 'g' stems in the 'small letters' section of this alphabet, to find out about their sexual energy level and fantasy).

Sharply angular in appearance:

In an intimate relationship, you can be sure this person will rapidly assume a position of dominance and control, and will exhibit a highly aggressive, self-righteous nature. If such people's position of power is questioned, they are liable to become extremely angry and argumentative, and you can be sure they will use cruel, sharp criticism to undermine a mate's self-esteem and confidence in order to strengthen their own authority.

If you see this sign in someone's writing, check the rest of this book for other indicators of aggression, and in particular, check the 'g' section of the alphabet to see if their aggressive behaviour affects their attitude towards sex.

INDIVIDUAL SECTION

VARIATIONS OF CAPITAL LETTERS THAT REVEAL INFORMATION RELEVANT TO SEX AND RELATIONSHIP

THE CAPITAL LETTER 'E'

Resembles a backward-facing number three:

Egg Every Eddy

Assuming he has the time and the leisure, this person will certainly be an avid reader. Those who form their capital 'E's in this way possess a sense of culture, and a desire to express themselves creatively, but if they find no suitable outlet will sublimate this drive by enjoying other people's artistic endeavours via theatre, art exhibitions, concerts, etc. To be happy in a relationship, this person will need a cultured partner who knows how to appreciate the finer things in life.

THE CAPITAL LETTER 'J'

With a balloon-shaped stem that is very noticeably extended to the left:

John J JJ

This person has a very sensitive, introspective nature, and there is a fair chance that there may be latent homosexual tendencies. See the small letter 'g' with stem extending to the left, page 102, for a full description of the person in whose writing this characteristic appears.

THE CAPITAL LETTERS 'K' AND 'R'

Arms form a sharp angle, piercing the stem:

It is very probable that in the distant past this person was hurt badly in some way by a member of the opposite sex, who was consequently strongly resented. Unresolved hostility for this person, now buried deep within the subconscious, sometimes precipitates in such people an attitude of generalized contempt for the opposite sex. When in this mood, they are likely to behave in an unreasonably antagonistic manner towards their partners, who become scapegoats for the unexpressed, frustrated angry emotion they have been feeling for so long. At times they are capable of being cuttingly hurtful to their mates, who may be on the receiving end of a barrage of esteem-destroying complaints and criticism.

A man with this trait often harbours a deep-seated (possibly subconscious) resentment for his mother, as well as for women in general, and he may be inclined to complain to his partner about domestic inefficiency, or insufficient sex drive.

A woman with this trait may have a grudge against her father, or some other man who has damaged her in some way. A general mistrust and dislike of the male of the species has made her rather unkind at times in her manner to her lover, and this may well reveal itself in taunting remarks aimed to belittle his work, or question his virility and skill in lovemaking.

Arms form a loop around the stem:

An essentially loving and warm, affectionate nature would be a fair description of this person's behaviour, if involved in a relationship that is at least fairly satisfying. There will, however, inevitably be a feeling of insecurity if the relationship does not include an abundance of mutual warmth and sensitivity, on both emotional and physical levels.

In lovemaking, these types will always appreciate it if plenty of time is devoted to kissing, cuddling, stroking and erotic foreplay, prior to the more advanced stages of full sexual intercourse. A woman with this trait, especially, will be left feeling very dissatisfied if her partner rushes this side of things.

Arms form a loop on the left-hand side of the stem:

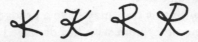

When someone with this characteristic is involved in an unsatisfying relationship, there will frequently be an attempt to escape this painful situation via flights of fancy, in which the person journeys back through time, to re-experience the love and harmony enjoyed with sweethearts of years gone by.

If a mate is sexually boring, such people are likely to shut their eyes during moments of lovemaking, in order to superimpose over their current experience the highly erotic sensations they remember from those gratifying encounters of the past.

Alternatively, they may simply mentally substitute some other fantasy ideal lover, such as a film star or musician, for the present partner.

Arms form either a loop or a half-circle and lightly touch the stem:

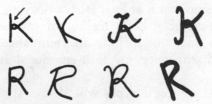

A person with this trait needs abundant affection and plenty of tactile stimulation to feel secure in a relationship. Perhaps insufficient warmth was received in childhood, and as an adult this person is seeking to fulfil this early need via a partner who enjoys equally all the touching, hugging and physically warm contact that comes with a satisfying and compatible relationship. After lovemaking, these types will like to linger on, in the comforting sensations of a lover's arms, drifting off to sleep in the temporary bliss of total security.

Such people will clearly be very distressed if they are living with someone who cannot give them the physical human warmth and contact they so desperately need for their peace of mind.

For a woman with this characteristic, an evening spent with her partner filled with affectionate kissing and cuddling, rather than lovemaking, will often be all that is needed to satisfy her desire for love and tenderness.

Arms detached from the stem:

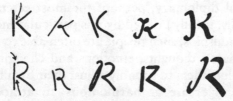

This person will think things through extremely carefully before becoming intimately involved with a potential partner.

If therefore, you are intending to start an intimate relationship with someone like this, you would be well advised to take things very slowly, as such people also seem to have an underlying fear of the sexual act.

Although they may enjoy a kiss and a cuddle, when the intimate foreplay begins they are likely to feel rather uneasy and embarrassed. Because of this apprehension they experience with regard to close physical contact, they can at times seem quite cool and distant in their manner towards a mate. To overcome any uncertainties they may have, they will clearly need an understanding, sensitive partner who can provide them with plenty of warmth and reassurance.

THE CAPITAL LETTER 'M'

Diminishes gradually in height without losing legibility:

Monaco Mandy

The art of diplomacy, perhaps the most essential of all social skills, is fully utilized by this particular individual.

In relationships, such people are often able to accurately sense a mate's thoughts, emotions and changing moods, thus enabling them to suitably adjust their own behaviour, in order to create as harmonious an atmosphere as possible. Being tactful, they will rarely, if ever, intentionally offend or upset their lovers, and great pains will be taken to resolve any arguments or conflicts as peacefully and quickly as possible. If however, they have done their best to calm the air, but without success, then to avoid making the issue worse, simple withdrawal and avoidance will generally be the chosen tactic.

It is not in such a person's nature to make social blunders or cast blame on others, and should an embarrassing situation occur every effort will be made to smooth things over, either by rendering the matter insignificant, or if possible acting as though it had not been noticed.

In lovemaking, as long as these people have a reasonably healthy sex drive, they will tend to be at least fairly sensitive, and are likely to do their best to satisfy their lovers' needs. They may have a tendency however, to use their insight into human nature, in combination with their capacity to communicate without arousing friction, in order to subtly gain the upper hand in a relationship. They are often able to cleverly manipulate the 'voluntary' co-operation of their mates, so that when it comes to decision making it is they who will be 'calling the shots'.

Unless there are negative signs elsewhere in the writing, there is every chance that this person will achieve a fair degree of harmony in an intimate relationship, unless of course there are obvious signs of incompatibility elsewhere in the relationship.

THE CAPITAL LETTER 'T'

Crossbar at least twice as long as the stem or a crossbar which slopes upwards:

An exceptionally strong will is one of the main features of this particular personality. Because of a natural instinct to lead others, in a relationship such people have a tendency to be too assertive and headstrong at times, and will inevitably try to make more than their fair share of the decisions. If living with a passive mate they need to make sure not to become bossy, domineering and self-righteous. If a mate also has strong leadership inclinations there is likely to be significant conflict, unless mutual agreement is reached as to how responsibilities will be shared, so that there is no competition for control.

When in a good mood, this person can be exceptionally passionate and enthusiastic in lovemaking (unless other factors in the writing indicate a low sex drive). When spirits are high, even if a mate is feeling down and not really in the mood for sex, there is every chance that the optimism, enthusiasm and energy this individual is capable of generating will be sufficient to restimulate in the unwilling lover a passion, once again, for living and loving.

Crossbar slopes noticeably downwards:

This individual has an extremely over-assertive, headstrong nature, and in an intimate relationship is frequently inclined to be excessively domineering. To feel satisfied with anyone, such a person will need to be boss, and if resisted will become very irritable and attack the sensitive spots in a partner's ego, in order to weaken self-esteem so as to gain submission. This unpleasant behaviour probably stems from being constantly criticized and judged in childhood by an overbearing, forceful parent. The desire for control is a futile effort to escape underlying feelings of inadequacy arising from this treatment. Much conflict and argument is inevitable if such a person's mate has the strength of personality to oppose this attempt at domination.

In lovemaking, if a man with this graphological characteristic also has a strong sex drive, he will become very easily frustrated if his sexual wishes are not gratified, and it is possible this may even lead to his using physical strength in order to compel his mate to submit to him.

If a woman with this writing sign is dissatisfied with her partner, she will inevitably be a classic example of the 'nagging type' who will take every opportunity to complain to her man about his failings, and if she finds him boring in bed, she may well punish him by depriving him of sex on all but very rare occasions.

If, however, she has a healthy sex drive, and is pleased with his lovemaking skills, she may well turn out to be very forward and uninhibited in sex, the type who will issue precise instructions as to which erotic positions should be employed, and she is unlikely to shy away from explaining exactly where, and how, she likes to be touched.

4. Small Letters

GENERAL SECTION

HANDWRITING THAT CAN APPEAR ON ANY SMALL LETTER

LEAD-IN STROKES

> **Many letters with a curved line attached, that droops clearly below the baseline:**
>
> *and then he turned away again*

This person has a strong 'tribal instinct' that leads to a feeling of insecurity when not attached to some sort of group. Such people feel a desperate need to get along with everyone around them, and will do their best to conform to the particular standards of those with whom they associate, in order to avoid any conflict or confrontation.

Their manner is generally very warm, responsive and sympathetic, and genuine compassion will be felt and shown if either a mate or someone they know is suffering or in trouble in any way. Having a very sentimental nature, they are always prepared to offer their lovers or close family and friends a shoulder to cry on, but they need to guard against becoming overly affected by other people's personal problems.

In relationships such people are likely to be sensitive and romantic, but could well have a tendency to overindulge in self-pity, whenever life treats them badly. Family ties will matter enormously to them, which may be a source of constant irritation to any mate who prefers a private one-to-one relationship, free from the influence of family, and especially in-laws. People with this graphological characteristic never fail to lend a helping hand if a close relative is in need. Indeed, many such individuals are, in spite of this, even prone to feelings of intense guilt that they are not doing enough. It is very possible that this 'guilt trip' originates from early childhood, when either they lived in an atmosphere of parental conflict or perhaps there was some other form of great suffering or sadness in the home.

Whatever the cause, they somehow felt strongly responsible for the situation, or maybe just very guilty that they were undeservedly better off in some way. Obviously such emotions would have been triggered off, or at least reinforced by other family members. As a consequence of all this, they often seem to allow others to take advantage of their good-natured desire to help, and may find themselves frequently imposed upon. Sexually, these types need to be shown an abundance of warmth and affection in order to feel really secure their mates love them.

A woman with this sign is likely to be very passive sexually, in the sense that even if she does not feel like making love with her partner, she will do so just to please him. She is unlikely to initiate any new approaches to lovemaking as she will tend to be insecure about trying out anything adventurous she might think of, in case it is not appreciated.

She will however be happy quietly to go along with whatever her mate might suggest, though she might not feel entirely at ease with anything too original, as her personality is likely to be founded upon quite conventional and conformist values. Generally, women in this category are sexually far more turned on by romance and warmth than by mere sexual adroitness and virility.

A man with this graphological characteristic will certainly not be nearly as passive as a woman with the same sign, owing to his considerably higher level of testosterone (the male hormone that influences both the sex drive and aggressiveness).

He will, however, usually go out of his way to please his mate sexually. If she is not in the mood for sex, even if he himself is highly aroused and ready for it, he will tend to be considerably less pushy about making love than the average man would, under the same circumstances. Like his female counterpart, he will tend to let his lover take the lead, with regard to creative, imaginative lovemaking, for he is unlikely to have a pioneering spirit when it comes to exploring new sexual horizons, preferring to stick to the 'tried and tested' approaches that have worked well for him in the past.

Many letters with a slightly curved or flexible line attached, that starts from the baseline or above it:

I saw him going along the beach

Being very much a creature of habit, this person will become highly insecure if anything upsets the status quo. Such individuals will only feel at home in an intimate relationship with someone fairly conventional who allows them to lead a structured, well-organized and fairly routine existence, so that they know exactly what is expected of them at any given moment. They would be thrown completely off balance by, and certainly not be happy with, any partner who is changeable, temperamental, or wild in any way.

Disliking sudden surprises or changes that oblige them to make spontaneous decisions or alter their normal pattern of living, these unadventurous spirits definitely need plenty of time to carefully plan and prepare themselves prior to starting something new or embarking on a journey of any sort. Being resistant to change, their attitudes will inevitably be rather rigid and traditional, for most of their opinions about life were fully formed a long time ago, and they are unprogressive and highly sceptical towards any new or innovative ideas. People with a personality structure of this type tend to be incredibly boring in bed, for their rigidly patterned manner of thinking and living invariably destroys their imagination and spontaneity in lovemaking.

A man in this category will have an approach to sex that is routine and monotonous with no surprises whatsoever, so his lover will always know exactly what is coming next. Each stage of foreplay will proceed in an infuriatingly predictable fashion, and even when it finally comes to full sexual intercourse, he will somehow still manage to maintain the same level of predictability: the duration of the event, his erotic talk or sexual grunting, and even the number and style of his thrusts will seem almost identical at each session.

To break him out of this rut, he will need an exceptionally imaginative and highly sexed mate, who has a personality that is strong enough to take complete charge, so as to lead the way into new and exciting sexual terrain.

A woman with this graphological sign, like her male counterpart, is also very robót-like in her approach to lovemaking. Invariably she will be highly passive, happy to let her lover take the reins whilst receptively accepting whatever lies in store for her.

Being very conventional at heart, she will appreciate any

sexual activity that remains well within the confines of whatever is considered to be the sexual social norm. In spite of this, she is unlikely to offer much resistance if her lover pushes her to indulge in erotic play that lies far outside this boundary. Instead, such women tend to reluctantly and quietly accept their fate in such circumstances, no matter how unpalatable they might find the demands. When such a woman discovers a pattern of reacting to her mate's sexual behaviour which pleases him, she will tend to adopt this same approach during every single session. The sexual patter used to turn him on will almost always be identical, and the sounds she makes signifying her arousal (whether genuine or not) will always have the same pitch, rhythm, frequency and duration. At the end of the whole process, if a genuine orgasm fails to occur, you can be quite certain she will hide this fact with a very realistic imitation of an extremely satisfying peak experience.

A woman with this trait will only overcome her excessively routine approach and passivity in this area if she is fortunate enough to find a highly sensitive and understanding man who does not take unfair advantage of her sheep-like nature and desire to please. He will need to slowly and carefully help her to believe that she is loved and accepted for what she really is, rather than what she thinks she ought to be. In this way, she should be able to gradually break free of the chains of fear that restrain her, in order to liberally express the desires and natural spontaneity of her true inner personality.

UPPER STEMS

Looped stem close to the central zone:

This person has a vivid imagination that frequently seems to focus on the more humorous side of existence. This healthy perspective on life gives an ability to see the comic nature of circumstances even when faced with problems or misfortune. In social situations such people really enjoy a good laugh, and when necessary can be relied upon to relate an amusing anecdote or crack a joke to lighten the atmosphere.

Establishing new relationships will not be too difficult for them as they have charismatic appeal and a smooth, witty style of conversation that should attract a fairly wide variety of potential partners. If conflicts arise with a mate, they will sometimes be able to resolve them remarkably quickly as their light-hearted manner will often have the effect of transforming any vibrations of tension into laughter.

For further information on the sexual behaviour patterns and other aspects of personality connected with this graphological characteristic see 'The Humorous Lover', page 268.

Looped stem that is consistently narrow or retraced:

I had the feeling I was falling down

A strait-jacket of fear is restricting considerably the free expression of this person's potential in many areas of life. Imagination is being strongly suppressed and the scope of thought has been narrowed to include only that which synchronizes easily with what is already known. Long-established opinions and attitudes, and old tried and tested solutions to problems form the familiar, but severely limiting, fabric of this character's existence.

The lack of receptivity in the minds and hearts of such people slows the evolution of their consciousness and blocks their inner growth. They are tough-minded, and will ignorantly stick with old attitudes that may be harmful, rather than letting go and allowing a newer, and more positive perspective to develop.

In relationships their sceptical, dismissive reaction towards anything innovative or different is liable to frequently upset and irritate their partners. Also, being emotionally repressed, they find it almost impossible to freely express their feelings, and this could cause a lack of openness in communication. This blocked personality probably originates from an overly strict and repressive childhood, which stifled this individual's self-expression and creative impulses. From this arose low self-esteem, as well as a tendency to strong feelings of guilt. These people's fearful nature could also stem from certain traumatic events in their early years, which they might have excluded from memory.

WORD ENDINGS

Cup-shaped ending (must be at the end of a word to be valid):

and hid though am at are

When you enter this person's home you will not need to wait long before you are asked if you are hungry or thirsty, for this graphological sign shows a generous heart and someone who certainly knows the meaning of hospitality.

On social occasions such people will often be the first to reach for their money, and will usually be prepared to pay more than their fair share, as they gain pleasure from being generous, especially if they are out having a good time with friends. In a close relationship, they will generally be sensitive, good-natured and understanding, considerate enough to sense when something is wrong.

In lovemaking, therefore, there is a reasonable chance that they will turn out to be considerate of a mate's feelings and needs, and with their naturally generous nature they are bound to make the necessary effort to satisfy their lovers sexually. This characteristic will help them considerably in achieving harmonious relationships, as their partners will undoubtedly respond very warmly to such an open-handed personality.

**Ending rises noticeably high (must be at
the end of a word to be valid):**

and are though gum fun

A generally optimistic spirit guides this particular member
of the human race on the journey through life. When
misfortune strikes, an inner faith that everything will turn
out fine in the end helps such people recover quickly, and
they may even manage to see something of value in the
situation. They enjoy talking to people, and their *joie de
vivre* can be quite contagious. Their relationships will be
enhanced by their positive attitude, and their passion for
life will help to neutralize any depressive or pessimistic
moods that may overcome a partner.

People with this graphological characteristic are capable
of being quite passionate and enthusiastic in lovemaking
(unless other factors in the writing indicate a low sex
drive). When they are in one of their optimistic states of
mind, even if a mate is feeling unhappy and therefore not
really in the mood for sex, there is every chance that the
enthusiasm and energy they are capable of generating will
be infectious enough to restimulate in an unwilling lover a
desire once again for the sensual pleasure of sexual
satisfaction.

**Ending is sharply angled and ascends diagonally
(must be at the end of a word to be valid):**

And can nut at though

A rigid and uncompromising attitude makes this person
sceptical and unreceptive towards other people's ideas and
opinions. In relationships, he or she will want to play the
lead role, and if a partner does not accept this, criticism and
complaint will be resorted to in an effort to maintain the
upper hand.

Their judgmental and highly critical nature will often
make such people unpleasant to live with, and they are
likely to lack those elements of romance and softness that
enhance the more intimate side of human relationship.
Being very self-critical makes it exceptionally difficult for
them to accept themselves, and this often seems to close
their hearts to the emotions of compassion and
understanding that are so necessary for achieving a deep
sense of connectedness with another human being.
Consequently the manner of their lovemaking is unlikely to
leave a lover with that warm, secure, loving glow that can
make all the troubles of the world temporarily melt away.

INDIVIDUAL SECTION

INDIVIDUAL LETTER-SHAPE VARIATIONS OF SMALL LETTERS THAT REVEAL INFORMATION RELEVANT TO SEX AND RELATIONSHIP

THE SMALL LETTERS 'a' AND 'o'

Nearly always very rounded and clear inside:

good food as always

There is a reasonable chance that this person may actually turn out to be sincere and straightforward, candid in opinions and honourable in commitments.

This is one of the graphological characteristics that often appear in the handwriting of people who turn out to be very faithful to their partners in an intimate relationship. In addition, these types are usually quite romantic at heart, though they may choose to hide this, for fear of being hurt.

Often quite sensitive and warm in their approach to lovemaking, they will usually be able to express their feelings of love fairly easily, and will do their best to make a mate feel safe and secure during the whole process. (Unless of course there are other obvious signs in the writing which negate the positive effects of this graphological sign.)

With a dangling line inside the circle:

going on and on **one day away**

At the moment this person is preoccupied with worries about sex. This may be due to an absence of it, or he or she may be dissatisfied with some aspect of sexual performance. Whatever the reason, the symptomatic tension that is being experienced as a consequence of frustrations in this area could well cause him or her, from time to time, to lash out at a mate with rather cutting remarks.

Noticeably larger than other letters in the central zone:

dog year doing eat cane

This characteristic always indicates someone who feels uncertain of a partner's affection. Such people are often emotionally very demanding, as they expect a great deal of attention from a mate, and if they do not receive this they can become very hostile.

They possess a naturally rebellious streak, and are also inclined to become very insecure on social occasions, if a partner appears to be paying a great deal of attention to other members of the opposite sex. In such instances, there is a fair chance that they will later confront a mate with an outburst of jealous anger. (See 'The Jealous Lover', page 296, for other graphological signs that confirm such behaviour.)

THE SMALL LETTER 'd'

Stem is a single, ascending line:

dog grade day dim

See 'The Capital Letter 'E'' on page 73 for a description of the person in whose writing this graphological characteristic appears.

Stem at least four times the size of the central zone:

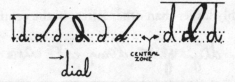

A strong desire to gain approval and respect from society has made this individual over-concerned with personal appearance and prestige. If at times such a person seems to be a little vain or perhaps conceited, remember that this is merely a thin facade that hides deeply rooted feelings of inadequacy, formed during early childhood.

Living with people like this will not be easy. Their troubled minds and poor self-esteem can sometimes make them very self-obsessed and egocentric, and when this happens they will become very insensitive towards other people's needs and feelings.

In lovemaking, a man with this trait will desperately want to make a good impression on his partner, and will therefore be extremely self-conscious and tense with regard to his performance. Unless the woman he is with supplies him with plenty of adulation and reassurance, either verbally or via highly pleasurable sexual reactions to his lovemaking, he will feel he has been inadequate. Indeed, where his virility is concerned, he will inevitably be extremely vulnerable to any criticism. Any lover, however, who is skilled in the art of sexual compliments may find herself well rewarded for her efforts, as men with this graphological sign are likely to be especially stimulated, both mentally and physically, by any well-chosen sexual praise.

Women with this sign in their writing are also highly self-conscious, but unlike their male counterparts are far more concerned about their physical appearance than their performance.

A woman with this trait is likely to worry excessively that her body is not sufficiently appealing, or alternatively, if she is very confident of her sexual charisma, then the chances are high that she will have an exaggerated fear of losing this appeal as she grows older. In a long-term intimate relationship, she will always be on the lookout for any signs in her partner's sexual behaviour which signal a reduction in his arousal or interest when he is in bed with her; if she spots any such indications, she is likely to become insecure about her appeal for him.

With looped stem (the loop must not be wider than the central zone):

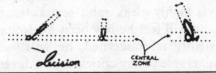

Accurately sensing the thoughts, feelings and mood of a mate is not difficult for this human being, who can establish a rapport with others remarkably quickly, even on a first meeting. Unless there are other obvious signs in the writing of darker aspects of personality that could neutralize the positive effects of this trait, then this person is likely to be a sympathetic listener, capable of showing warmth and understanding in a relationship.

If such individuals have a healthy desire for lovemaking, then this trait will serve to enhance their style of foreplay as it will help them synchronize their own movements with the rhythm, responses and needs of their lovers.

Finally, if someone is living with such a person, they would do well to remember that this sensitive nature is very vulnerable, and can easily be hurt by criticism or negative vibrations.

Looped stem at least twice as wide as the central zone:

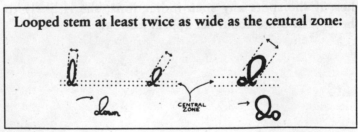

Over-sensitivity to criticism is the cause of a great deal of suffering in this person's life. Excessive care about the opinions of other people causes bruising of the ego, and an in-built 'radar' allows the detection of even the subtlest of personal attacks. Such hypersensitivity is clearly a handicap in relationships, as well-meant advice will sometimes be considered a put-down, and even silence itself may at times be misinterpreted as unspoken disapproval.

Such people will become incredibly upset and angry if a mate makes the bad mistake of openly attacking and criticizing them, and if their writing has a muddy appearance, slopes strongly to the right, or has other signs indicating a lack of emotional self-control, then they may lose their grip completely, and react in a physically violent manner. (A man with this trait is more likely to demonstrate physically aggressive behaviour than a woman with the same sign. There is both a cultural and physiological basis for this difference, which is explained in detail in 'Are You In Danger?' page 216.)

The disturbed personality structure of people with this graphological characteristic can probably be traced back to a childhood plagued by frequent criticism or unreasonably high parental expectations. This has created a guilt complex in the personality as well as an intense fear of rejection, and the interaction of these two neurotic characteristics has produced the current persecution complex.

On the positive side, such individuals are likely to have a very sentimental facet to their nature, and if treated only with kindness and good vibrations, they are capable of being extremely warm and sensitive (unless of course there are other signs in the writing showing negative aspects of human nature that will prevent this potentially good side from expressing itself).

Such types are often capable of sensing other people's

thoughts and feelings with uncanny accuracy, and in an intimate relationship, as long as there are no serious conflicts blocking communication, they can be exceptionally good-natured, understanding and considerate. In lovemaking, however, they can be prone to worrying far too much about the quality of their performance, as they are bound to have strong fears of not being able to impress and please a lover.

A man with this trait will generally be over-concerned about the quality of his lovemaking skills, and will harbour fears that perhaps he does not match up to other lovers his mate may have had in the past. He will only feel confident in his sexuality if his lover shows very visible signs of pleasure during sexual intimacy, and any criticism in this area is likely to damage his sexual ego severely and could easily impair his prowess. Any compliments about his style of lovemaking, however, will be music to his ears, and act as a powerful aphrodisiac that is sure to enhance the quality of his sexual performance. His lover therefore is likely to be amply rewarded by such well-chosen praise.

Women with this sign in their writing, unlike their male counterparts, are more concerned about their physical appearance than their performance. They are often very insecure about their looks, and sexual charisma, and invariably harbour exaggerated fears of the degenerative changes in the human body that inevitably occur with the passage of time. They dread what they consider will be a fading of their femininity and sexual attractiveness, together with all the negative side-effects this may have on the quality of their relationships as well as their social status.

Such a neurotic woman tends to be constantly on guard for any signals that might indicate a change in her lover's interest in her. Even if her mate finds her irresistible, she may still suffer from a paranoia that makes her imagine the contrary. In such cases, the consequential unwarranted fears about her sexuality and physical attractiveness can become an obsession that is capable of severely impairing the quality of a relationship.

Stem detached from the round portion:

Bed doing *bread* steady

This handwriting sign applies to women only.

This woman likes to flirt, and arouse a man's passion by making him believe that she really fancies him. But if he makes a pass, it may well be turned down. She does this not out of desire to hurt or tease but simply because she is insecure about her femininity, and needs to confirm to herself and others that she is still appealing to the opposite sex.

Stem forms tent-like shape:

dog and pad idea

Opinionated and obstinate, is an accurate description of this particular character, who will vehemently argue to defend a point of view; quite definitely this is not the sort to fall obediently into line and blindly follow orders.

Such people have an inwardly rebellious nature, and a distaste for being told what to do, so great friction is guaranteed if they are involved in an intimate relationship with anyone domineering or over-assertive.

If you are living with someone like this, and need permission before taking a certain course of action, do not propose the subject in a manner that allows the person to answer yes or no. Once people with this graphological sign decide against something, then they are frequently disinclined to change their minds, even if they feel at a later stage that their decision was in fact wrong. The only way to get a proposal passed, when you are dealing with such stubborn human beings, is cleverly to manipulate them into thinking that the idea was theirs.

People with this trait will need to learn the meaning of the word compromise if they wish to avoid much unnecessary unhappiness in their relationships. When things do not go their way, they can become very irritable and difficult to live with, but on the positive side they generally have the courage of their convictions to stand up for what they believe in.

Stem leans far more to the right than the rest of the writing:

intended collected found

On meeting this person for the first time, you could easily be forgiven if you failed to notice an extremely volatile temperament. Attempts at self-restraint have precipitated an oscillation between extreme over-control on some occasions (which may possibly create the illusion of emotional balance) and almost hysterical outbursts of anger or frustration at other times.

Quite clearly, a pressured life style should be avoided at

all costs by such people, for it is stress, strain and tension which provoke the complete loss of psychological equilibrium leading to the neurotic emotional eruptions. They are very vulnerable to negative emotional atmospheres, and simply cannot tolerate any form of hostile behaviour from others, and so anyone who dares to cross them will certainly live to regret it. There will be regular shouting matches if a partner offends them, or lacks emotional self-control, but on the positive side, if treated well, they can be extremely loving, romantic and passionate.

A love life with such an individual will be a real roller-coaster ride. Sometimes, in those rare moments when the relationship is running smoothly and there is a flow of mutual good feeling, lovemaking may well turn out to be absolutely fabulous (assuming the sex drive of both parties is reasonably normal). Under such conditions, this individual is capable of radiating tremendous heartfelt warmth and powerful sexual passions, and so the style of foreplay and lovemaking is likely to be intense, exciting and full of the freshness of spontaneously expressed loving feelings.

At other times, however, when such a person's mood takes a sharp and sudden swing for the worse, and communication channels are disrupted by dark, stormy emotions, there will be little or no chance of any form of sexual intimacy occurring, as the atmosphere will be filled with fiercely expressed anger, and even hatred.

Indeed, if there are other signs in the writing of poor emotional self-control, revealed perhaps by muddy writing or writing with a confused restless appearance, then this anger may even take the form of physically violent outbursts. Such people would be well advised to seek help in controlling their over-emotional nature.

THE SMALL LETTER 'e'

Resembles a backward-facing number 3:

egg meal Easy pet

If this individual's life style permits, then during leisure time a temporary escape will be sought from all the worries of the world, by just stretching out on a comfortable sofa or bed, whiling away the hours engrossed in a book.

In an intimate relationship, this may turn out to be a source of conflict, as sometimes such people may become so absorbed by a piece of exciting reading material that they will even ignore the sexual advances of a mate.

Luckily there is a perfect solution to this problem if you happen to be living with someone like this: simply supply some well-written, erotic literature, and even if this captivates your mate's full attention do not worry, as sooner or later his or her libido is bound to become so aroused that sexual fiction will in no way be able to compete with real-life erotic experiences.

THE SMALL LETTER 'g'

Stem has a smoothly curved balloon-shaped appearance (not less than the height of the central zone, but not more than one and a half times the height):

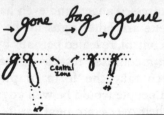

This individual's warm, friendly, enthusiastic manner will help to maintain a friendly rapport with others both at home and in the outside world.

In courtship, people with this characteristic will usually be quite sensitive to a partner's state of mind, and with their ability to talk well, and listen with enthusiasm, they will certainly be a pleasure to have around.

Even on a first night out, they will have no trouble in rapidly breaking the ice to make their partners feel as comfortable as if they were with an old acquaintance they had known for years.

In an intimate relationship which is sexually satisfying, they could well turn out to be a warm, loving human being capable of finding contentment in life with just one partner. They will, however, become easily frustrated if they are living with someone who is insufficiently receptive to their sexual advances, and under such circumstances, they may begin to look elsewhere to satisfy their sensual appetites.

For further information on the sexual behaviour patterns and other aspects of personality connected with this graphological characteristic, see 'The Considerate Lover', page 264.

With an over-inflated balloon appearance of any shape (the stem must also be at least two and a half times the size of the central zone):

An abundantly vivid imagination and extreme intensity of desire has given this individual an unquenchable thirst to live life to the full. An intimate relationship with this person will never be dull, but the tension at times may become excessive as there is a tendency to juggle far too many goals simultaneously, which stresses and complicates existence unnecessarily. In addition, a limitless erotic fantasy and strong libido makes such people extremely demanding in love, so in long-term relationships it will be exceptionally difficult to keep them sexually satisfied for any significant length of time. If the balloon-shaped stem is very noticeably extended to the left, see 'I Wonder... Straight or Gay?' page 205 for clear graphic examples and an interpretation of this variation.

For further information on the sexual behaviour patterns and other aspects of personality connected with this highly significant and extremely dominant writing sign, see 'The Sex-Crazy Lover', page 249.

Consistently extremely narrow loop:

Individuals with this graphological characteristic are filled with intense fear and insecurity, and have a very low sexual self-assurance. This will, however, not necessarily be evident to others, as most people in this category hide such facts about themselves behind a well-constructed wall of secrecy. Socially, these types are self-conscious and inwardly ill at ease, and will rarely exhibit any relaxed, spontaneous behaviour unless they happen to be alcohol-intoxicated. In relationships, deeply rooted sexual inhibitions strongly undermine the quality of their sexual experiences and prevent them from establishing a sense of connectedness with their partner.

Although sexual inhibitions can stem from a number of possible causes, the problem in this case is almost certainly rooted in a pronounced inferiority complex, and repressed sexual feelings, originating in early childhood.

For further information on the sexual behaviour patterns and other aspects of personality connected with this highly important graphological characteristic, see 'I Could Never Do This With My Partner!' page 196.

Stem consistently retraced (upstroke traces downstroke, forming one line):

gong giggle angling gag

When this graphological characteristic is seen in someone's writing, the behaviour patterns mentioned for the previous graphological characteristic (where the 'g' stem is consistently extremely narrow) apply here, but are greatly accentuated.

Retraced stems on the 'g' indicate someone who is very severely repressed, and in addition there may be a blocking out from the memory of some childhood or early teenage trauma (possibly sexual in nature) that the person was unable to come to terms with. People with this graphological characteristic possess an unusually private, secretive nature, and are ultra-cautious of people in general. Even those intimate with them are unlikely to ever come anywhere near to the inner sanctuary of their hidden thoughts and feelings. In addition, they invariably also have obsessive compulsive tendencies. This graphological characteristic may also indicate sexual dysfunction, e.g. premature ejaculation in men or frigidity in women.

People with consistently retraced stems in their writing should seek professional help in order to overcome the repressive tendencies in their personality, which may otherwise impair their physical and/or psychological health.

For further information on the sexual behaviour patterns and other aspects of personality connected with this highly important graphological characteristic, see 'I Could Never Do This With My Partner!' page 196.

With a sharply angled triangle of any shape:

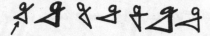

During the early stages of courtship, even if this person appears to be perfectly charming, be on your guard! The moment such people feel they are firmly established in an intimate relationship, they are very likely to become extremely self-righteous, fault-finding and tyrannical. They certainly do not have a balanced, healthy attitude towards love and sex, and this will inevitably be an additional source of conflict, in any relationship.

For further information on the sexual behaviour patterns and other aspects of personality connected with this very significant graphological characteristic, see 'The Tyrannical Lover', page 291.

End of stem sharply angled:

$$9 \quad 9 \quad 9 \quad 9 \quad 9$$

If you see this sign in someone's writing, you can be almost certain you are dealing with a person who is deeply unfulfilled, with both career and intimate relationships, though such feelings will generally be kept hidden.

In social situations such an individual will be tense and uneasy, but will attempt to conceal this from others, possibly behind a facade of formality and aloofness. Much anger is being bottled up in this personality, and some of it will inevitably find expression in the private world of any long-term intimate relationship.

These types often feel a sense of inner isolation and loneliness, and even if they are living with someone who clearly loves them, they may still find it difficult to believe that they are genuinely appreciated. This condition is reinforced, or perhaps precipitated, by their fear of really letting go during lovemaking, as this hinders them from achieving a close union with their mates, both sexually and emotionally. Consequently, their sex life is likely to be very dissatisfying and will cause them a great deal of frustration. They may well blame their partners for the unhappiness they are experiencing, and if so, will undoubtedly harbour feelings of deep resentment towards them. In such cases, this will reveal itself through domineering, judgmental, uncompromising attitudes, esteem-destroying criticism, bad temper, and moods in which they sulk and ignore their mates completely.

Strangely shaped stem that forms two loops:

If you are thinking of entering into a relationship with this person, then it is absolutely essential that you first find out exactly what their sexual preferences are. Perhaps it may be possible for you to meet up with a previous long-term partner who would be in a position to provide you with the necessary information. If you fail to follow this advice, whilst continuing with this relationship, you could be in for a shock, unless you happen to have similar sexual tastes.

The presence of this sign in a person's writing definitely does not indicate a conventional attitude towards sex. Indeed, such people can only really enjoy lovemaking if they are indulging in certain highly unorthodox practices which are incompatible with the sexual repertoire of most heterosexuals. Their erotic imagination is filled with images of themselves gaining sexual satisfaction in ways which most people in society still find somewhat unacceptable.

Many people with this sign in their writing feel a strong attraction towards members of their own sex, and if so, there is a good chance they will indulge themselves physically in such desires on an occasional, or even regular, basis. In some individuals, however, this tendency is strongly suppressed, becoming a dormant potential that may, or may not, emerge at a later stage in their lives. In such cases, the person might well attempt to lead a normal heterosexual existence. Eventually, however, the build-up of intense emotional and sexual frustration may prove to be too difficult to handle, and if this happens the individual will either terminate the heterosexual existence completely, or simply lead a double life, indulging these emotional and sexual needs in total secrecy. See 'I Wonder...Straight or Gay?', page 205.

Shaped like either a number 8 or an elongated 'S'

ᶦ ſone ſot gum ſive grill

This cultivated, highly intelligent, literary-minded individual has artistic potential and a strong sense of culture. To find satisfaction in a relationship, such a person definitely needs to be with someone who has a compatible intellectual make-up.

Such people appreciate lively discussions, and will quickly tire of any mate who is less knowledgeable, is slow-witted or is lacking in culture, as their agile, penetrating minds crave abundant stimulation.

To remain sexually attracted to someone throughout a long-term relationship, therefore, it is essential that this person finds not only a physically attractive mate but one who is also intellectually exciting.

Such people's approach to lovemaking will sometimes be refreshingly light-hearted, as they have a distinctly humorous streak in their personality and can often see the comic nature of existence. When this witty side of the personality is active, it will obviously help to clear up any disagreements they may have with a mate.

Many people who have this sign in their writing possess a good intuition or 'sixth sense', that allows them to perceive with great accuracy other people's thoughts and feelings. In a close relationship with a partner they trust, such individuals can be capable of great sensitivity and understanding. They will know how to listen sympathetically and will always sense when something is troubling a partner.

However, the positive traits described in this portrait

will rarely express themselves in the personality if there are also negative signs in the writing, such as 'The Whip', see page 44.

Ascending line completed, but remaining far below the central zone:

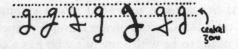

This person's mind is often filled with unpleasant memories of the past which, for various reasons, are kept absolutely private. If you are the type who likes easy-going individuals with wide-ranging social tastes, then this character is certainly not a suitable choice.

Socially, such people will always gravitate towards like-minded personalities, preferring to keep their circle of friends to a very select few. Their somewhat rigid, inflexible thinking makes them inwardly ill at ease, especially when they are with people who are different in terms of personality and attitudes.

A person with this sign in his writing is likely to feel isolated, lonely, unappreciated and physically unattractive, and at the time of writing may be going through a period of emotional and sexual deprivation which is causing a great deal of frustration in both these areas. There is a small chance that this state of affairs may be temporary, perhaps caused by a recent break-up of a relationship. When the person finds someone else, the problems may vanish. Alternatively, a series of unhappy experiences could cause constant anxiety with regard to sexual and emotional involvement.

Such individuals are unable to 'drop their guard', and

thus cannot open themselves to a partner emotionally and sexually. If the stem of the 'g' forms a tiny round loop at the bottom (as in the last example opposite) then the writer is likely to seek out some sort of release from his tension through very frequent masturbation. Unless this situation is resolved, a relationship with this person is unlikely to be very satisfactory.

In bed, such people will be unspontaneous, inhibited and tense, and their style of foreplay and lovemaking is therefore bound to be unimaginative and stilted. Unable to let go into the flow of feeling, they will have at best only very weak orgasms and their partners will inevitably also leave the show feeling very dissatisfied and sexually frustrated.

As with most psychological problems however, these people's emotional and sexual fears can be overcome if they seek the help of a suitable professional therapist.

Ascending line not completed:

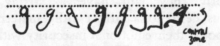

This person is 'hung up' on the past, sometimes being absorbed in thoughts of happier days gone by, and on other occasions overwhelmed by memories of various sad events.

There is a strong possibility that previous relationships have been particularly painful and unpleasant, and this has made the person disinclined to face up to the realities of the present. Some people with this characteristic are particularly attracted to alcohol or drugs which seem to offer a potential escape from life and all its problems.

Emotionally and sexually, there are strong feelings of

unfulfilment and frustration, and such people seem to lack hope that the unsatisfactory condition of their sex life will ever alter for the better. Many of them feel a sense of uneasiness whilst lovemaking, and are unable to relax sufficiently to tune into their own, or their partners' sexual needs and feelings. Frequently they are late developers emotionally and sexually, and it is their immature attitude to sex and relationship that is ruining the quality of their experiences.

If the ascending line forms a 'cup shape' as in the first example, the childlike side of this person's nature is still quite intact, and therefore in an intimate relationship, definite signs of emotional immaturity will be shown in attitudes, expectations and behaviour. This type of formation (which is often seen in the handwriting of teenage girls) often indicates a romantic but unrealistic attitude to life and emotions.

Such individuals usually have very ambivalent feelings towards their mothers, stemming from a childhood where they may have felt neglected or insufficiently loved. Consequently they will have a strong, possibly subconscious, desire for a partner with a maternal instinct, who can soothe their emotional insecurity with plenty of tenderness and affection. They themselves are capable of being very gentle and loving at times, and there is a very good chance that they will communicate excellently with children, as they have the knack of being able to get on the same childlike wavelength, by playing as an equal, rather than as an adult.

With a line ascending to the right resembling the letter 'q':

gone fig age giving

If you are on the lookout for someone who is a real rock in times of crisis, then the odds are in favour of this person being exactly what you are after. Being practical-minded and realistic, as well as conscientious and efficient, such people show abundant initiative and can make quick, sensible decisions. Even when under high pressure they will not ever completely lose their 'cool'. In an intimate relationship, they will definitely appreciate being the one who has the final word, as they invariably seem to be very confident that they know the best course of action for any given situation. Rather judgmental and critical of any inefficiency and laziness, they will expect everything in the home to be 'ship-shape', running smoothly and according to plan.

Unfortunately, however, these people find it difficult to switch off their overwhelming need to control life as much as possible, and this tends to make them very stressful, and consequently neglectful of their own and their partners' sexual needs.

For further information on the sexual behaviour patterns and other aspects of personality connected with this graphological characteristic, see the description of personality relevant to Point 3 in 'Foreplay? Who Cares?', page 183.

**With a line ascending to the right resembling
the letter 'q' and a rounded base:**

give right dog night

Sympathetic and understanding, this person has an altruistic streak and is clearly capable of being very warm and considerate in relationships. He or she is, however, not expressing sexual energy in the normal fashion, and may well be suppressing and redirecting it via other channels, such as work. Tension and conflict is likely to arise in the sexual sphere of the relationship, if such a person is living with someone who has normal, healthy sexual needs.

For further information on the sexual behaviour patterns and other aspects of personality connected with this graphological characteristic, see 'The Sublimated Lover', page 259.

**Descending line at least three and a half times the size
of the central zone. (This point is not valid if the 'g's
are written with a pen pressure that is very light, faded,
or weak in appearance.)**

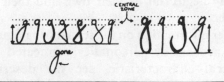

Energy, determination, and a strong sex drive are characteristics which aptly describe this particular individual. These types are usually very active and productive, but no matter how busy they become, sex is likely to always remain high up on their list of priorities.

For further information on the sexual behaviour patterns and other aspects of personality connected with this very significant graphological characteristic, see 'The Potent Lover', page 243.

Descending line at least four and a half times the size of the central zone. (This point is not valid if the 'g's are written with a pen pressure that is very light, faded, or weak in appearance.)

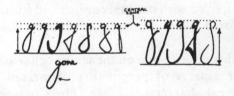

When the descending line of the letter 'g' reaches this length, it reveals someone with an enormously high level of energy and determination. Indeed, such individuals are invariably over-adrenalized and over-ambitious, as well as hyperactive and restless. In relationships they will be very difficult to live with, as they have workaholic tendencies, and find it difficult to sit back and relax. In addition, people with this graphological characteristic have unbelievable sexual stamina, and become very easily frustrated if they do not have a partner who enjoys making love on a daily basis.

For further information on the sexual behaviour patterns and other aspects of personality connected with this highly significant and extremely dominant writing sign, see 'The Potent Lover', page 243.

Stem overlaps with the line below:

*going along the gangway
all along the watchtower*

Physically minded, sensual and intense, this person has loads of determination, energy and ambition, as well as strong creative impulses. Unfortunately though, many individuals with this graphological characteristic achieve little of their potential in life, as they are at war with themselves, filled with internal conflict and frustration that has confused their thinking and complicated their existence.

For further information on the sexual behaviour patterns and other aspects of personality connected with this graphological characteristic, see 'The Confused Lover', page 282.

Descending line consistently short (not longer than the height of the central zone). The writing must be light in pressure, and clean, not smudgy or smeary in appearance, or with ink-filled ovals. There must be no examples of 'g's which have a large balloon-shaped stem.

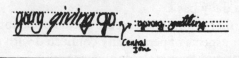

again we are going to go along

going giving go going getting

Central Zone

This person's choice of mate is unlikely to have been influenced by matters such as financial status, as people with this graphological sign are surprisingly un-materialistic (so long as they do not have balloon-looped 'y's in their writing).

Their physical vitality, however, is low, and they will probably have a poor libido which could easily lead to sexual incompatibility if they are involved in an intimate relationship with someone who has a healthy sex drive.

If the stem is so short that it barely descends below the baseline, this person is likely to be suffering from problems of impotence. If this is the case, see 'This Has Never Happened To Me Before!' page 190, for further details.

For further information on the sexual behaviour patterns and other aspects of personality connected with this graphological characteristic, see 'The Occasional Lover', page 256.

Descending line appears pulled to the right:

going swing fighting

Living with this person certainly will not be easy, as this graphological characteristic invariably reveals a restless workaholic. These types rarely devote sufficient time to their relationships, and this may well leave partners feeling neglected and unloved and also sexually dissatisfied. Stressful and overworked, they need to take great care that they do not drive themselves into a state of psychological and/or physical ill-health.

For further information on the sexual behaviour patterns and other aspects of personality connected with this graphological characteristic, see 'The Workaholic Lover', page 285.

Only a descending line:

gone bag hug dig get green

Concerned primarily with the practical affairs of everyday living, this person tends to have a responsible attitude to life and its obligations. A matter-of-fact approach and emotional self-control help such a person to maintain perspective and keep a cool head, even when things become hectic and stressful.

These individuals' manner to others, although generally polite, is likely to be somewhat formal and restrained, and their choice of close personal friends will be highly selective, and kept to an absolute minimum. They will clearly not be the ideal mate for anyone gregarious, as in their leisure time they would usually far rather remain at home engaged in an activity of their choice, than go to a party or involve themselves in any other light-hearted social activity. Indeed their idea of a wasted evening is time spent in superficial socializing with casual acquaintances, for they have a naturally cautious nature that prevents them from feeling at ease with anyone whom they do not know exceptionally well. Treasuring their privacy, they will, whenever possible, seek out moments of solitude to balance the time they spend with others.

When it comes to the area of sex and companionship, the head very much rules the heart in such people. At the start of a new relationship, it will take them quite a while before they allow themselves to open up at all emotionally. They often tend to restrain any sexual attraction they may feel towards people they have only recently met, until they have had sufficient time to assess fully whether or not the person concerned would make a suitable partner. Somewhat rigid in their views, their manner of communication is usually very direct, and in an intimate relationship they can be quite critical and judgmental of a mate who behaves inappropriately. They rarely turn out to be considerate lovers, and are therefore unlikely to be attentive to a mate's needs and desires.

If the descending line becomes sharp like a needle point at the end, then in addition to all of the above, men and women with this characteristic will at times be harshly judgmental and critical. When they are angry, or if they are simply in a bad mood, they can be cuttingly sarcastic and skilful in using their sharp tongues in locating the most vulnerable areas of the ego. They find it impossible to 'forgive and forget' if someone crosses them, but will conceal such grudge-bearing emotions from all but those who know them exceptionally well.

For further information on the sexual behaviour patterns connected with this graphological characteristic, see the description of personality relevant to Point 2 in 'Foreplay? Who Cares?', page 183.

Stem forms an 'Eagle's Talon':

This graphological sign indicates someone who often suffers from feelings of dissatisfaction and sexual frustration, and in addition may well be insensitive to a partner's feelings and needs. Consequently, it is likely that such a person will be very demanding and difficult to live with.

In relationships these types usually attempt to establish

119

a position of control over their mates, and you can be sure they will want to be the one who determines how much money is spent in the home. Economically minded, they are the sort who value, and count, every penny that is spent, and they will become overly upset if there is any expenditure which they deem unnecessary.

Even if such a person's outer appearance should turn out to be conventional, you can be certain that underneath this is an individual who is at heart a rebel, capable of unconventional or even eccentric behaviour. Sexual tastes will almost definitely be unusual, and there may well be a taste for kinky eroticism, though it is possible this fact will be hidden from lovers.

For further information on the sexual behaviour patterns and other aspects of personality connected with this graphological characteristic, see 'The Eagle's Talon', page 34.

Base of stem is missing and a cross-shape is formed:

This graphological indicator is a sure sign of a disturbed sex life and relationship. This person tends to be permanently sexually frustrated and dissatisfied with any partner. Many people with this trait have a tendency to change partners very regularly, as even if they enjoy someone's company and find sex satisfying during the early stages of a relationship, they quickly become discontented and restless, and are liable to look elsewhere, in the hope of finding a compatible lover.

Some people with this graphological sign suffer from

frequent bouts of sexual impotence, and in such cases any promiscuous behaviour is likely to be motivated by the temporary relief from this problem that they perhaps find during the excitement of new sexual encounters. You should therefore also check the writing for any of the graphological signs contained in 'This Has Never Happened To Me Before!', page 190.

Over-inflated balloon-looped stem very noticeably extended to the left:

This person has a very sensitive, introspective nature, and may have latent homosexual tendencies. Many individuals with this trait have not yet freed themselves from their early emotional attachment to their mothers. Even as adults, these types relate to their mothers (or the memory of their mothers if they are no longer alive) in a manner reminiscent of a very young pre-pubescent emotionally dependent child. Consequently, they are likely to harmonize best in a relationship with someone who is prepared to treat them in a protective, caring maternal manner.

If you come across this sign in someone's writing, this by no means suggests the person actually leads a homosexual or bisexual existence, as the tendency may be completely repressed. It is therefore vital, before jumping to any hasty conclusions, that you refer to 'I Wonder...Straight or Gay?', page 205.

Ascending line of the stem forms a loop, and then droops downwards below the baseline:

g g g g g g g g

This graphological sign is an indication of despondency or depression with lovemaking. The person is going through a period in which there is very little satisfaction from the potential pleasures of lovemaking. This may be due to pressures and stresses from work, or perhaps from some recent personal misfortune. Alternatively, there may be anger and resentment towards a mate as a result of conflicts in the relationship. The lower down on the stem the loop, the deeper the resentment and dissatisfaction. Using 'What's the Score in Bed', page 303, check this person's writing and his or her partner's to see if the current problems stem from differing sexual appetites.

Ascending line moves in the reverse direction to form a loop:

g g g g g g g

This characteristic frequently signifies a rebellious streak, and it is therefore very likely that this person has a very independent way of thinking and a self-styled manner of living that could well include behaviour patterns that are highly unconventional.

These types easily become bored as they need constant stimulation, and their sense of humour is likely to be very different from the norm. In lovemaking, they are likely to have unusual tastes and will therefore find conventional approaches to lovemaking rather unexciting and unstimulating. If this graphological sign is seen in the writing in combination with certain other graphic features, latent homosexual tendencies may possibly be present, so you should carefully check with the information in 'I Wonder...Straight or Gay?', page 205.

THE SMALL LETTER *'i'*

> **Circle over the 'i' instead of a dot:**
>
> *it is incredibly interesting isn't it*

This sign in a person's writing indicates a need and desire for more attention than is currently being obtained. Even a celebrity with this sign, in spite of abundant recognition and popularity, will not feel satisfied, and will still try to get more. Such people are often emotionally immature, and may well manage to maintain a teenage mentality, even much later on in life.

In a relationship these people will become deeply distressed if a mate fails to pay regular attention to them as they need constant praise and reassurance to compensate for a deep sense of emotional insecurity, that can invariably be traced back to a disturbed childhood that left them feeling insufficiently loved or appreciated.

These types often have strongly creative inclinations, and usually want to be seen as different or unique in some way. This characteristic often appears in the writing with other graphological signs indicating narcissistic behaviour. You should therefore check with 'Everybody, Look At Me! Am I Wonderful?', page 227.

At least half the 'i's have dots missing:

it is a pity it didn't fit

If you are involved in a personal relationship with this person, don't be upset if your birthday or anniversary is forgotten. It is not due to selfishness; quite simply he or she is absent-minded.

Such people should take this problem seriously, by making a conscious effort to unify their minds with their bodies when performing any action, however mundane it may be. Otherwise countless hours are liable to be wasted in the process of looking for keys, contact lenses or glasses etc., or trying to remember where the car was parked.

One final word of warning; in an intimate relationship with this person, if it is important for you that a condom is used during lovemaking, then make sure you are the one who is responsible for remembering this. If you are foolish enough to rely on this individual to always carry this necessary article, then you are likely to be sorely disappointed, as even with matters as important as this, this very forgetful character could easily let you down. Consequently, during a moment of passion when you are on the brink of beginning full sexual intercourse, you may find you both have to take a cold shower instead, as the necessary item is not at hand.

> **Dot is very close to and directly above the stem:**
>
> *if it is interesting*

An uncanny eye for detail and the capacity to focus the attention single-mindedly on one thing at a time have given this individual a remarkable memory. Indeed, many people with this characteristic can recall specific events, even from early childhood, as vividly as if they had occurred the previous day.

If such people happen to have a romantic streak, then they will be the sort who remember the precise details of where and when they met their lovers, and during moments of nostalgia will have a clear recall of virtually every loving romantic moment they ever experienced in their lives.

They will appreciate a home environment that is orderly and tidy, and being naturally fastidious will find slovenliness or disorganization in a partner difficult to tolerate, as they need everything to be running 'ship-shape' in order to feel relaxed. Sometimes though, they take things too far, and can become increasingly petty and pedantic, unnecessarily fussy and over-concerned with the significance of trivial matters.

If however, they happen to be sexually aware, and fully realize the special importance of the whole process of foreplay, then this faculty they possess for paying detailed attention will prove to be a great asset. If they so choose, their ample patience and fine mental focus will enable them to slowly travel around a lover's body, giving complete and loving attention to each erotic zone in turn, whilst noticing and responding to all the subtle nuances of a mate's reactions, until he or she reaches a peak of pleasurable arousal.

Dot is consistently small and round:

investigation is limiting his rights!

Unless there are obvious signs in the writing that suggest otherwise, if this person is your friend there is a reasonable chance that you will meet with sincerity, straight-forwardness and candid opinions.

Generally speaking, you can trust such people to be reliable and faithful to their commitments, as they usually have a sense of honour and an ethical attitude towards friendship and its obligations. Simultaneously however, they will be very hurt by broken promises or unreliability, and will find it very difficult to overlook and forget such incidences.

This is one of the graphological characteristics that often appears in the handwriting of people who turn out to be very faithful to their partners in intimate relationships.

THE SMALL LETTER '*m*'

Diminishes gradually in height without losing legibility:

time lime

See the description given on page 78 of the person who shows the same characteristic in writing the capital letter 'M'.

> **Sharply angled at top and bottom:**
>
> *man met him mud map*

This person is independent minded, highly opinionated, and has a penetrative, intelligent manner of thinking.

In relationships, there is a strong possibility that such people will misuse their sharp analytical brains for the purpose of judging and criticizing, and they will often be unnecessarily rigid in their viewpoints. Once their minds are made up about something, there will be a complete absence of receptivity to any alternative ideas a mate might have.

In lovemaking, these people sometimes tend to stand outside of themselves, watching carefully, and are inclined to be inwardly very critical of their performance.

If a man with this trait also happens to have a very high sex drive, then he is likely to become very judgmental and even verbally abusive towards his partner if she refuses to make love as often as he would like. In such instances, he may well try to destroy her self-esteem by criticizing her sexual performance and physical appearance, in a misguided attempt to coerce her into surrendering to his sexual demands.

> **With rounded tops, the last noticeably higher:**
>
> *more man frame drama aim*

A fragile ego has made this individual over-concerned with making a good impression on others. Highly self-conscious, and suffering constantly from a fear of losing poise and being negatively judged, if such a person makes a mistake or seems clumsy in any way, he or she will therefore feel acutely embarrassed in other people's company.

The roots of this type of neurosis can probably be traced back to a childhood where the person felt undervalued or rejected by a parent, sibling, or possibly even teachers or classmates. Being unable to live up to the expectations of others, such people often develop a poor self-concept, and a tendency to worry that people will not accept them for who they really are.

Gaining plenty of admiration and respect from a mate will be essential to them, as without this the quality of any relationship will suffer considerably, and this will inevitably also have negative repercussions in the bedroom. Due to their emotional insecurity and fear of rejection, they will need to be constantly reassured of a partner's love.

The virility of men with this trait is extremely vulnerable to criticism. Indeed, if a man with this graphological characteristic is living with someone who lacks respect for him, there is a fair chance that he will lose his confidence in bed to such an extent that he will at times be unable to get an erection, or alternatively may suffer from other problems such as premature ejaculation.

Conversely, however, a lover who is prepared to pay him some suitable sexual compliments will probably be well rewarded for her efforts, as men in this category seem to be especially stimulated, both mentally and physically, by well-chosen sexual praise.

Women with this sign in their writing tend to be more concerned about their looks than their sexual skills. They invariably worry about their sexual appeal and are often prone to exaggerated fears about the degenerative changes in their physical appearance that will be caused by the ageing process. Such a woman is always on the watch for any signs which point to a reduction in her lover's sexual arousal or interest: if she notices or imagines any such indications, she is likely to become desperately insecure about her sexuality and attractiveness.

The last top is noticeably higher and sharply angled:

m̃ m̃ m̃ m̃ m̃ m̃

This person is likely to be self-righteous and quarrelsome and very awkward to live with in an intimate relationship. In discussion, even with little knowledge of a subject, he or she will try to pretend they are an authority on it. This disagreeable behaviour is simply a futile attempt to escape deeply rooted feelings of inferiority. Such people are self-conscious and their feelings of inadequacy are coupled with fears of being negatively judged by others. In lovemaking they are likely to be over-concerned with the quality of their performance and what their partners think of them as lovers, and this is bound to interfere with the pleasure they gain from the act.

Lines are retraced and the letter has a cramped, compressed appearance:

m m m m m m m m

This person is emotionally repressed, and highly secretive with regard to innermost thoughts and feelings, which are likely to be hidden even from those who are closest.

Such people's lives are ruled by numerous fears that are the product of their highly insecure nature. Bottling up their feelings and suppressing numerous desires and urges, they rarely lose their tempers, but if they do the outburst is likely to be very explosive. This writing sign often appears together with the graphological signs of sexual repression, so you should check for this possibility with 'I Could Never Do This With My Partner!', page 196.

Final stroke curls back to the left underneath the letter:

m m m m m

People whose writing shows this graphological sign are usually very materialistic, and may well have a tendency towards greediness. They possess a fighting spirit, but unfortunately this is also likely to affect their intimate relationships, in which they can demonstrate a very hot temper and an inability to talk things over and compromise. They often turn out to be very selfish and intolerant in their treatment of partners, and it is therefore very unlikely that they will turn out to be considerate lovers.

THE SMALL LETTER 'O'

(Except for the example below, the interpretations of this letter are the same as for the letter 'a'.)

Loop frequently crosses over at the top:

good to see you this morning!

This sign is an indication of unreliability. People in whose writing it appears often turn out to have a detached and rather cold and unaffectionate manner in their relationships; they are secretive, and may also be deceitful.

Look, however, for other signs in the writing that confirm this.

THE SMALL LETTER '*p*'

Over-inflated balloon-looped stem:

Balloon-looped 'p's indicate exhibitionist tendencies and an excessive concern with physical appearance. People who show this sign, generally speaking, have a great love of sport and other physical activities, as well as a healthy sexual appetite. This graphological characteristic often appears in combination with other features indicating narcissistic behaviour. You should therefore check the writing for the signs given in 'Everybody, Look at Me! Am I Wonderful?', page 227.

THE SMALL LETTER '*t*'

Crossbar slopes noticeably downwards:

This person has an extremely over-assertive, headstrong nature, and in an intimate relationship is frequently inclined to be very domineering. This behaviour pattern is likely to express itself in all areas of the relationship, including sexual behaviour.

For further information on the sexual behaviour patterns and other aspects of personality connected with this graphological characteristic, see 'The Domineering Lover', page 289.

Crossbar on the right, detached from the stem:

at hot get hit - but too

This person frequently experiences feelings of impatience, but with good self-control may manage to hide this from those who do not know him or her exceptionally well. Such a person's mind is usually several steps ahead of events, and there is often a tendency to worry a lot about the future.

What makes matters even worse is that people like this are inclined to take on much more than they can comfortably handle, thereby causing trouble to themselves and those around them. They intensely dislike superficial chit-chat, and find long-winded or verbose talkers unbearably irritating.

In relationships they can be short-tempered, especially if they encounter any form of aggression or delay. They need to learn to slow down more and relax into the present, so that they do not rush themselves and their partners, as this creates a great deal of pointless stress in the home environment. To help matters, their mates should make extra sure that they are not kept waiting when something needs to be done.

Because human beings are creatures of habit, any established pattern of behaviour will tend to express itself throughout many different areas of the personality. Consequently, the impatient nature of people with this graphological characteristic generally affects and pollutes most of their existence, including their love life. Indeed, it is very rare that an individual with this characteristic is a good lover, for such types have a tendency to hurry sex, and therefore fail to allow sufficient time for the very important sensual prelude of foreplay.

For detailed information on the sexual behaviour patterns and other aspects of personality connected with this graphological characteristic, see the description of personality relevant to Point 1 in 'Foreplay? Who Cares?', page 183.

Crossbar fractionally below the top of the stem, and nearly as long as, or longer than, the stem:

best it hat met

If you see this sign in someone's writing, then it is very likely that he or she is highly ambitious and full of plans for the future. Unfortunately there is a grave danger that such a person will aim too high, and experience continual frustration as a result of futile attempts to achieve the unreachable.

A relationship with one of these characters is obviously not going to be easy, as if they are devoting so much time to ambition they are unlikely to be very attentive to their partners' feelings and needs. In addition, their tendency to expect so much from life could well influence their attitude towards a lover, and they may become excessively demanding and expect too much.

No crossbar and no variation of one:

what is that question time goes too fast

Like the writer who habitually leaves the dots off the letter 'i', this person is forgetful. For a fuller description, see page 124.

Crossbar floating above the stem:

not right what is this to you?

This person is at heart an idealist with very high aspirations, but can be difficult to live with. Such people are sometimes so absorbed in hopes and dreams for the future, that they lose touch with daily reality and find it difficult to concentrate on the needs of the moment; consequently they are frequently absent-minded.

When life is treating these types well, they can be very romantic towards their mates, and excited and enthusiastic in their approach to lovemaking, but when things go wrong the disappointment they experience is often so intense that they become totally preoccupied with their problems, to the exclusion of all else, including sex.

Crossbar at least twice as long as the stem:

tea too tip it

An exceptionally strong will is one of the main features of this particular personality. In addition, this individual has abundant enthusiasm and energy as well as a clearer idea than most about what he or she wants out of life.

In an intimate relationship, such people will automatically try to take control of decision making, as they have a strong desire to lead others, and certainly need full control over their own actions, as they will not tolerate being told what to do.

They will often become very domineering, and will need to learn how to tone down this assertive nature, or else their more passive partners are liable to consider them unreasonably headstrong, bossy and self-righteous.

If however, they have a mate with an equally forceful nature, major conflicts in communication are unavoidable, and this could have devastating effects on their sex lives. In such instances, negotiations will need to be undertaken, leading to mutual agreement as to the division of responsibilities, so that there is no competition for control.

As long as they have a reasonably healthy sex drive, individuals with this graphological characteristic are likely to be exceptionally enthusiastic in their manner of lovemaking.

If however, a man with this writing sign happens to also have a strong sexual appetite, then there is a distinct possibility he might use his highly assertive nature to force himself on to an unwilling partner.

Crossbar forms star-shape to the left of the stem:

nut hat got pet

An unreasonably obstinate, inwardly rebellious, headstrong nature will make it very difficult for this individual to tolerate anyone in authority. Such people simply cannot stand anyone poking a nose into their business or telling them what to do. They will become exceptionally angry if anyone attempts to criticize or dominate them in any way, and there is a strong possibility that they will try to manipulate themselves into a position of power in the relationship, where they themselves are in the controlling seat.

These types are rarely a pleasure to live with, as when they are in a bad mood, they can be very irritable and sharp-tongued, and in such instances are quite capable of bombarding their mates with esteem-destroying criticism that will not easily be forgotten.

PART TWO

Doodles

5. Introduction to Doodling

That old cliché, 'a picture paints a thousand words', is a wonderfully apt description of the potentially revealing nature of doodles. Almost everyone indulges in this habit, on the telephone at work or at home, or during board meetings, etc., but perhaps the best testimony to its widespread popularity is in the fortune spent each year on removing from numerous public places, doodles or 'graffiti', drawn in pen, pencil, lipstick and paint.

If you thought up until now that all those little pictures, scribbles and patterns were merely idle, meaningless movements produced by a bored or preoccupied mind, then you could not be further from the truth. To begin with, the repetition of lines or shapes typical of doodling helps to relax the mind, and thus the thinking processes become clearer and more effective. In addition, beneath the surface appearance of many a doodle lies an intimate story about its owner, for these revealing pictures are symbolic transmissions from the deepest levels of our being.

Since the days when Sigmund Freud and Carl Jung first realized that the source of almost all behaviour lies in our unconscious mind, doodles have been accepted as one of several potential means of plumbing these hidden depths. These two great fathers of modern-day psychology described the unknown area of our subconscious as being like a great oceanic expanse, as compared with the conscious part of the brain, which was likened to a tiny inland lake. They recognized that this deeper part of our being communicated its nature surreptitiously, via a coded language consisting of symbols, images and gestures rather than words, and that only by examining and interpreting this secret code could we hope to reach a full understanding of our innermost thoughts, feelings and motives.

As a result of these profound insights, psychologists, psychiatrists, graphologists and others in the field of personality assessment now devote considerable time to uncovering the meaning of the symbols and gestures of various important facets of human expression, including dreams, body gestures, handwriting and last, but not least, doodling. Indeed, interpreting the symbolic meaning of doodles formed part of the armoury of investigation used by Jung and Freud during their intrepid journey into the darkest recesses of the human psyche.

Sigmund Freud believed that the pictures or patterns we make in the process of doodling are often a disguised expression of repressed sexual traumas, or hidden sexual desires, frustrations or hostile feelings, which we find too shameful or disturbing to consciously acknowledge. By hiding such truths from ourselves, we protect our ego from guilt, and feelings of inadequacy or self-disgust that we might otherwise experience. This action of repression, however, causes a tremendous build-up of inner tension.

Freud felt that doodles (and also dreams) are vehicles which allow the mind to express these 'improper' thoughts and impulses, in a covert and acceptable manner; they act as escape valves, providing some sort of freedom and release to some of the blocked emotional energy festering in our subconscious. While the main beam of our attention is involved in some other activity, intense pent-up feelings of sexual frustration, and even violent emotions can be doodled away safely, without any disturbance to the status quo of our conscious mind, and the soothing effect this has on our nerves is considerable.

One needs to distinguish between doodles that are very rarely drawn, indicating either a very mild personality tendency, or a passing state of mind such as a brief mood of anger or depression, and doodles which are repeated, for these reveal dominant characteristics or tendencies that rule the individual's behaviour.

The same doodle repeated countless times on the same page may well indicate an obsessive compulsive state of mind. The person is frequently possessed by the thought pattern or emotion revealed by the doodle.

This chapter contains clear interpretations of all the doodles one is ever likely to come across that contain information about an individual's sexual nature. Alphabetically ordered and easy to use, this dictionary will instantly reveal the hidden meaning of any sexual doodle, bringing to light the person's erotic thoughts and feelings, or alerting you to the presence of hostile or even dangerously sadistic sexual impulses.

Classic graphological principles have been applied to the interpretation of the lines and shapes used in the formation of each doodle, and this information has been synthesized with well-founded psychological insight, in combination with the standard translations of doodle symbolism as provided by the research of Jung and Freud.

6. The Dictionary of Sexual Doodles

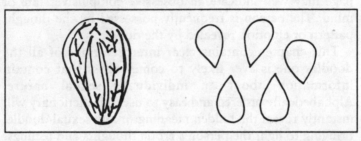

ALMOND: A female doodler is likely to be an adolescent girl or a virginal woman. The almond is symbolic of the vagina, and the fact that it has not been opened suggests a preoccupation with or self-consciousness about their virginity.

A male doodler views the female organ as a mystery, and is insecure about his ability to sexually arouse a partner.

ANGEL: Indicates a romantic and enlightened attitude to sex. Lovemaking is considered a mystical union, culminating in the orgasm which is seen as a fusion with the universe. If, however, the angel is heavily shaded or coloured black, then the above does not apply, and the person is suffering from feelings of depression due to shattered hopes and dreams. In a man, this doodle may also sometimes be an indication of repressed sexuality, and possibly latent homosexual tendencies.

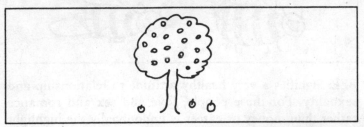

APPLE TREE: The individual feels very emotionally dependent. If the apples are on the ground, this shows underlying fears of sexual rejection.

AXE: See 'Sharp Weapons'.

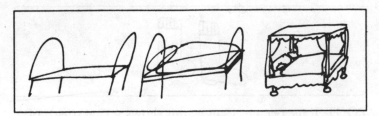

BED: If someone's habitual doodle is a bed, this indicates that sex is something which represents love, warmth and tenderness rather than wild, erotic lusts. The ritual of lovemaking is seen as a safe oasis and escape from the frightening hardships of existence and such a person will invariably be emotionally very dependent on a lover. Men who draw this doodle are likely to seek out a woman who has a very loving maternal manner, whereas women who draw it will search for a paternalistic figure to shield them from life.

BEE: Signifies a very healthy attitude to relationship and sexuality. For these people, love and sex and romance rather than money or career is undoubtedly the highlight of existence. They have the capacity to enjoy fully all the sensual pleasures of sex, and in bed they will be sensitive and considerate, and will undoubtedly pay full attention to all the niceties of foreplay. However, if the bee is feeding from a flower, look up under 'Insertion Doodles'.

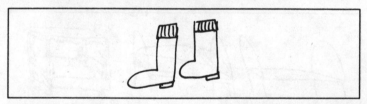

BOOT: If the person is single, this shows sexual frustration with recent relationships, and he or she is permanently preoccupied with meeting someone who is really hot in bed. If the boot has a very heavy appearance, this indicates a desire to dominate one's lover, both in the bed and out of it.

BOUQUET: A female doodler has romantic feelings towards her mate, and is sexually satisfied.

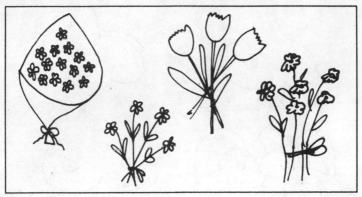

A male doodler reveals an underlying feminine sensitivity, and a willingness to do his utmost to give sexual pleasure to his partner.

BOWL: See 'Cup'.

BOW-TIE: A female doodler finds difficulty enjoying sex, unless she feels she is involved in a secure long-term relationship.

A male doodler reveals insecurity about his bedroom skills, so will need plenty of praise and reassurance.

BREASTS: A female doodler shows a strong dissatisfaction with the size of her breasts, and intense fear that men do not find this part of her anatomy sexually arousing. There may also be a desire for motherhood that at the moment she is repressing.

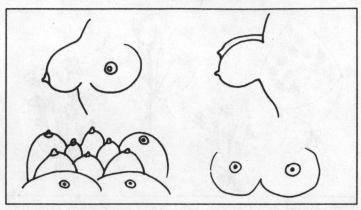

A male doodler is orally fixated, and obsessed with cunnilingus which for him is the indisputable high point of foreplay. Men who doodle breasts invariably have a very emotionally immature, childlike side to their nature, and are therefore very likely to be highly attracted to women who are prepared to sometimes treat them in a non-sexual, affectionate, caring, maternalistic manner.

BULL: A female doodler who habitually draws bulls generally has mixed feelings towards men who make love in a very tough, macho manner. They are torn between feelings of admiration and hostile resentment.

A male doodler typically has a strong sexual appetite, together with insecurity about virility, even if outwardly the doodler has a confident manner. If the horns of the bull are very long, this suggests great dissatisfaction with the length of the penis. If the bull has an unpleasant, aggressive appearance, this almost certainly points to feelings of sexual frustration, and resentment towards a lover.

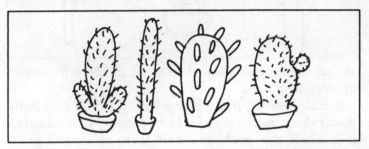

CACTUS: In a woman, this doodle is a sign of immense sexual frustration coupled with aggressive feelings towards a lover, and/or men in general. This person does not feel comfortable with the male organ and certainly does not enjoy handling it. She has a deep mistrust of men, and is fearful of sexual intercourse, which for her has connotations of pain rather than pleasure.

If a man makes this doodle, he has a hostile attitude towards the whole area of sex, which he may feel is dirty in some way. He fears losing control over his sexual impulses and will tend to feel disgusted with himself when experiencing sexual arousal. It is very possible that he will regard the penis as something destructive, to be restrained, rather than as an organ of pleasure.

CANDLE: A female doodler has a preoccupation or fascination with the male organ. A small candle may indicate a lack of concern about size, whereas a large candle reveals a strong preference for a penis that is large and thick. If the candle is drawn with wax dripping down the sides, then she may be experiencing immense sexual frustration, stemming from a repression of enormous and

147

almost unquenchable sexual lusts, which she is frightened of unleashing.

A male doodler, if this is regularly doodled, constantly thinks about his penis, and may be prone to erotic dreams. It is likely this problem stems from childhood guilt, connected with feelings of sexual arousal. Striving to suppress his natural sexual impulses, he caused his subconscious to produce instead this unnatural obsession with his sexual organ. If the candle is dripping wax down the sides, it is likely that he masturbates compulsively. The dripping wax may also point to repressed bisexual tendencies.

CANING STICK: See 'Whip'.

CANNON: See 'Gun'.

CAR: Almost exclusively a male doodle. If the car has a

very prominent exhaust, this is a phallic sign. Men who doodle cars tend to be obsessed with sex, and regard themselves as extremely virile. They are likely to consider themselves very well endowed, and will wait expectantly to be complimented in this area, whenever they meet a new lover. They thoroughly enjoy a varied sex life with many partners, as they are too self-obsessed and egocentric to devote themselves effectively to a long-term relationship. They cannot give up the buzz and excitement they derive from impressing new lovers.

CIGARETTE: A phallic symbol representing frustrated sexual feelings. If there is smoke rising from the tip, this shows the individual still has hope that his or her sex life will improve in the future, but if the smoke sinks, then subconscious feelings of depression and hopelessness prevail.

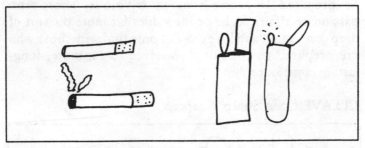

CIGARETTE LIGHTER: The sign of a one-track mind, that thinks of nothing but dating and sex. Often the type to frequent singles bars, this doodler is in search of exciting erotic encounters rather than serious relationships, and is inclined to change partners the moment something better comes along. A man who draws a lighter which has a dark, heavy appearance that makes deep indentations clearly visible on the reverse of the paper may be inclined to use physical force to coerce an unwilling mate into carrying out his sexual demands.

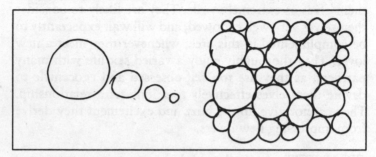

CIRCLE: Reveals an essentially sincere, kind-hearted, friendly individual who is likely to be faithful in relationships. The style of lovemaking will be warm and sensitive, and there will be no difficulty in expressing, as well as receiving, love and affection. This person will not be prepared to waste time in frivolous, short-term passionate affairs, as he or she values far more the sort of deep connection and love one can only find with those who are prepared to commit themselves to intimate, long-lasting companionship.

CLEAVER: See 'Sharp Weapons'.

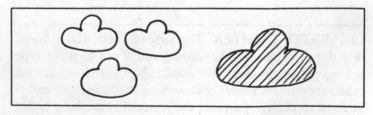

CLOUDS: Those who doodle clouds are not only sexually dissatisfied, but are also unhappy with their present life circumstances in general. In an attempt to escape the harsh realities of existence, these people tend to daydream about finding the ideal sexual relationship. If, however, the clouds are shaded, or black, this discloses a deeply depressed state of mind as a result of an especially unhappy sex life and relationship, which the person feels unable to cope with or escape.

COCK (the bird): The doodler is frightened of losing control over very intense sexual lusts.

CUP: A female doodler has warm-hearted feelings towards men in general, and an open-mindedness towards sex. Women who doodle cups are sensitive, kind and thoughtful and generally have a very straightforward, generous, sincere and uncomplicated nature. Being primarily motivated in life by a desire for love, rather than material wealth or wild sexual encounters, they are very unlikely to indulge in passionate one-night stands, financially motivated relationships, or brief love affairs based merely on sexual lust. They are instead looking for the close intimate companionship of a long-lasting, meaningful relationship based on love, and only if such conditions are fulfilled will they be able to fully express their extremely warm, sensual, and passionate sexual nature. The chances are extremely high that such a person will turn out to be a very reliable and faithful partner in life.

A male doodler shows feminine sensitivity, romantic feelings, and open-hearted generosity. The approach to lovemaking will be sensitive, thoughtful and uninhibited.

CUPID: Signifies a powerful desire to find happiness in a long-term relationship. These types usually have a strongly romantic, idealistic nature and are at times inclined to be in love with love.

DAISY CHAIN: See 'Flowers'.

DEVIL OR GARGOYLE: Suggests the strong suppression of very powerful sexual impulses and a fear that if these instinctive drives are allowed full rein, the doodler is in danger of behaving in a primitive and uncontrolled lecherous manner, like a wild animal possessed by its carnal lusts.

EYES: Often discloses a self-centred egocentric lover, so absorbed with the way life is treating him or her that anyone else's feelings are likely to be ignored. If the eyelashes are very prominent, see the meaning given below.

EYELASHES: A female doodler is very vain with regard to her physical appearance. She thoroughly enjoys flirting, but has strong feelings of apprehension when it comes to lovemaking. There is an element of mistrust towards men which prevents her from letting go during sexual intercourse. Consequently such women are usually sexually frustrated.

A male doodler has strong femininity in his personality. He is vain or even narcissistic, and there is a possibility he may be repressing bisexual tendencies.

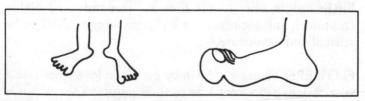

FEET: Signifies earthy, passionate sexual desires, and a straightforward, 'no beating about the bush' approach to lovemaking. People who make this doodle are not frightened to tell a lover what they want out of sex, but need perhaps to learn how to express their erotic desires in a manner that is a little more romantic.

FENCE: Indicates that sexual energies are being strongly suppressed. The doodler is sexually inhibited and unspontaneous, frightened of losing control over these primal instincts.

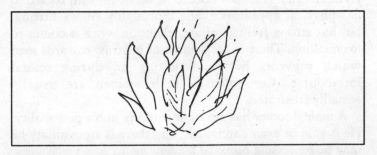

FIRE: People who doodle fires are romantic and highly emotional, and their manner of lovemaking is likely to be sensual and passionate.

FLOWERS: Typically drawn by people in love who have a very childlike innocent side to their nature. Their attitude to love, sex and relationships will be charmingly refreshing, though somewhat adolescent and immature at times. These

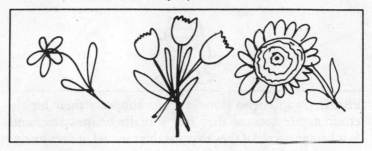

individuals are invariably very sentimental, compassionate and romantic, and are generally only able to really enjoy sex if it goes hand in hand with deep feelings of mutual love. This is certainly not the type who enjoys a passionately erotic one-night stand with a complete stranger. In a long-term relationship such people are likely to be loyal and faithful, and will undoubtedly be devastated if a partner deceives them with another lover.

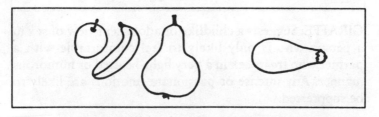

FOOD: Doodling fruit, vegetables and other types of food, is an indication of a warm sensual nature that hungers for a more satisfying sex life. Either the person concerned is not making love often enough, or if this is not the case, then perhaps their sexual experiences are simply not sensually gratifying. These types generally have a very healthy appetite for food and sex, and are inclined to erotic daydreaming, so their attitude to lovemaking is bound to be fairly open-minded. They will harmonize best with sexually active lovers who have a vivid sexual fantasy.

FROG: People who doodle frogs suppress their highly erotic nature because they feel sexually unattractive, and fear being rejected if they express their sexual desires freely.

GIRAFFE: Suggests a childlike or adolescent view of sex in a person who is only likely to feel comfortable with a partner who treats sex in a very light-hearted or humorous manner. Any intense or passionate emotions are likely to be suppressed.

GOAT: Signifies the presence of powerful sexual lusts that at present have not found an outlet. If the goat is drawn tethered to a post, then the person is being restricted for some reason from freely expressing sexuality. Perhaps he or she feels imprisoned in a sexually dissatisfying relationship, or alternatively the problem might stem from sexual inhibitions.

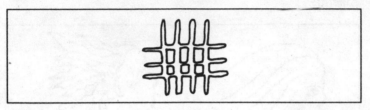

GRILLE PATTERN: Signifies sexual frustrations and tension. The doodler is finding it very difficult to relax and enjoy lovemaking, being constantly preoccupied with inescapable problems and responsibilities connected with daily survival. These people seem at the moment to be in a rut, which they are struggling unsuccessfully to get out of, and this is undermining their self-confidence and weakening their sexual self-esteem.

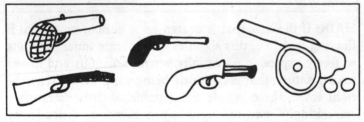

GUN: A female doodler may show hostile feelings towards a mate or a past lover, or even the male species in general. Alternatively, such women might suffer from penis envy or perhaps secretly wish they had been born a man, so that they could enjoy the powerful position they feel men have in society.

A male doodler shows underlying feelings of inadequacy

with respect to penis size, or sexual performance. Being so insecure about their virility, these types strongly suppress the more sensitive or feminine qualities of the male nature, and instead are inclined to present a front that is very macho.

HAIR: If the hair that is drawn on a human or animal is flowing and free, this signifies a desperate inner yearning to freely express a potentially warm, sensuous and loving sexual nature, that is currently being suppressed. With the right lover, these people are capable of demonstrating a refreshingly natural and open-minded attitude to lovemaking, free of the inhibitions and tensions inherent in most people.

Hair drawn in a style that is cut short, very sparse, or reminiscent of balding, indicates the individual concerned is not only sexually extremely frustrated, but also likely to suffer from strong feelings of inadequacy concerning some aspect of sexual make-up. This sexual insecurity may stem from strong underlying feelings of dissatisfaction connected with physical appearance or sexual performance. Men who doodle hair in this manner often harbour strong fears of losing their virility, and there may be a complex with regard to the size of the penis; women in this category are likely to be very insecure about their femininity and sex appeal, and are often very self-critical about breast or buttock size etc. Because of this basic lack of sexual self-respect, in both these cases, the style of lovemaking is likely to be tense and uneasy and lacking in sensuality and spontaneously expressed emotional warmth.

HEART: People who draw hearts invariably have a very childlike, innocent side to their nature, and so their emotional behaviour and approach to love and relationships is often reminiscent of a very young, teenage adolescent. Hearts that are gently curved rather than sharply formed at the bottom indicate a compassionate, warm and romantic sexual nature, possessing loyalty and a high regard for fidelity. If the heart is sharply angled at the bottom, the person will be highly judgmental, with a jealous streak, and the previously mentioned qualities will be instantly switched off if a mate does not conform closely to the required standards, especially in the area of lovemaking. For this type there is no such thing as romance without good quality sex.

A heart with an arrow through it indicates a childish, romantic, and compulsive daydreamer, who is in love with love. When involved in an intimate relationship, this doodler will be very jealous and possessive.

This doodle can also frequently signify unrequited love and sexual passion. If the arrow has a very pointed tip, then the disappointed emotions involved will be a mixture of anger, jealousy and depression, whereas a rounded tip on the arrow betrays only great sadness and regret, with no ill feelings towards the person who has ignored the doodler's love.

If the heart is divided into two or more pieces, this reveals severely depressed feelings due to a broken or unhappy relationship and sex life. Two hearts that overlap suggest harmony and love in the individual's sex life.

HORSE: A female doodler has excessive expectations in love. These women suffer from intense underlying feelings of frustration because they are too demanding when it comes to choosing a partner. He needs to be incredibly passionate and understanding, highly virile, and totally faithful. Anything less than this is not acceptable.

A male doodler may have strong emotions and unbridled sexual passions that he is afraid of expressing for fear of losing control.

ICE-CREAM CONE: Suggests tremendous hunger and

passion for sex, and high arousal by all the oral components of foreplay. Such people are highly sensual and are almost always ready for lovemaking.

INSECTS (excluding bees and butterflies): Doodling insects indicates an unhealthy attitude towards sex. These people suffer from guilt feelings, consciously or subconsciously, whenever they are gripped by erotic thoughts or feelings of sexual lust, and this has destroyed their ability to unashamedly enjoy the intense pleasure of sexual arousal and orgasm. Instead, during lovemaking they tend to 'separate' from the experience, observing it from outside whilst allowing feelings of disapproval or even disgust to diminish significantly the quality of the experience.

INSERTION DOODLES: Refers to any doodle incorporating pairs of objects in which one object goes inside another. The objects may be drawn either side by side or already connected to one another: Key and Lock, Train

with Tunnel, Bolt and Nut, Arrows and Quiver, Bee feeding from Flower, Lipstick protruding from its Holder, etc. Such doodles indicate tremendous sexual desire that at the moment is finding no satisfactory means of expression. Consequently, the individual is experiencing immense sexual frustration. Sometimes such feelings are denied and suppressed, in which case there will be no conscious awareness of the sexual tensions, and instead this frustrated energy will be diverted via some other channel such as an exaggerated interest in work or maybe a leisure activity such as horse-riding or motorbikes. The sexual troubles these people experience stem from external influences, for instance a current absence of any lover, or there may be argument and conflict in the relationship that has negatively affected the sex life. Alternatively, this sexual tension may be a result of a repressed sexual nature which is preventing this individual from freely expressing strong sexual impulses.

IRIS: Those who doodle irises spend much time thinking about sexual intercourse, and are inclined to have a sensitive, warm approach to lovemaking that is gentle, sensuous and romantic.

162

IVY: Invariably a doodle that signifies an individual's deep respect for the qualities of loyalty and fidelity. This is not the type who gets a kick out of casual sexual encounters.

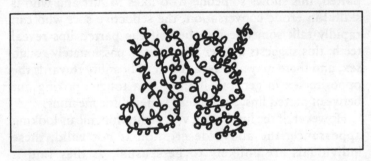

JAR: See 'Cup'.

JUG: See 'Cup'.

KNIFE: See under 'Sharp Weapons'.

LIPS: Symbolic of the lips of the vagina, this doodle indicates a strongly sensual lover who thoroughly enjoys sex. The larger and thicker the lips, the greater the sensual cravings. During foreplay, these types will invariably devote a great deal of time to passionate kissing, and they will almost certainly thoroughly enjoy giving and receiving oral sex.

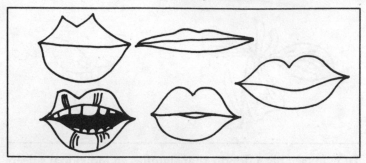

If the lips are closed, this indicates someone who will be very thoughtful and considerate in bed. If the lips are parted, this shows someone who likes to flirt and who is skilful in erotic conversation, the seductive sort who can rapidly talk someone into bed. If the parted lips reveal teeth, this suggests a lover who enjoys passionately rough sex, and there may also be a touch of hostility towards the opposite sex in general. If there is a tongue poking out between parted lips, see under 'Tongue' for meaning.

However, if the lips have a very tight, thin, mean-looking appearance, the above description is not valid; these individuals are unlikely to be sensual, as they find it difficult to freely express or receive heartfelt emotion and this impairs their ability to relax and enjoy the intimacy of touching, caressing and sensuous, deep kissing that is so necessary for satisfactory foreplay. Their style of lovemaking is therefore liable to be rather stiff, lacking in spontaneity and warmth. Drawings of tight, thin lips may also be a sign of problems in the relationship, perhaps an underlying hostility or resentment towards a lover, or even towards the opposite sex in general.

MACHETE: See 'Sharp Weapons'.

MOUSTACHE: Almost exclusively doodled by males.

Indicates insecurity concerning virility, and a desire to project to others a strong image of manliness.

NAMES: Those who doodle their own names frequently turn out to be too self-obsessed and egocentric to perform well in bed. In lovemaking they are rarely tuned into the sensual needs and sexual reactions of their partners, as they are usually over-concerned with what they are getting out of the experience. Men in this category also tend to overplay the importance of how virile or manly they appear to be.

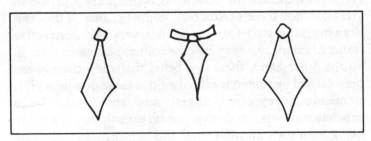

NECKTIE: A female doodler may have a desire to be accepted by men as 'one of the lads' rather than as a member of the female species. Alternatively, there may be repressed bisexual inclinations.

A male doodler, if the tie is very prominent, usually has strong feelings of sexual inadequacy or insecurity concerning the size of his male organ.

NEST: If there are eggs inside, a doodle of a nest almost always points to a highly aroused reproductive instinct. Whether the person is consciously aware of it or not, he or she desperately wants to start a family.

NOOSE: Indicates the doodler is undergoing a period of great conflict. If the person feels guilty because of this, this drawing suggests he or she is in a very self-destructive frame of mind, and may even be contemplating suicide. If, on the other hand, there is a belief that the situation has been caused by someone else, then this same doodle reveals tremendous repressed anger, and there may be a subconscious wish to do this person great harm. If you are living with such an individual and presently experiencing severe problems in the relationship, then be on your guard!

NOSE: If the nose drawn by a woman is very small, or sharply pointed, or drooping noticeably downwards, this could indicate the person is strongly dissatisfied with her lover's performance in bed. This same doodle sometimes suggests a certain hostility towards men in general. If,

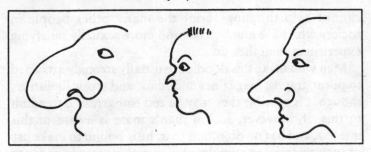

however, the nose is drawn with a rounded tip and points horizontally or upwards, this suggests fond feelings towards a mate, a light-hearted and open attitude towards sex and the male organ, and thus an enjoyment of lovemaking. If the nose is also extremely large, this may in addition reveal a strong fascination for the male organ, and a huge sexual appetite.

If a man doodles a small nose, this indicates either fears of impotence or concern that a lover may think his penis is much too small. A large nose shows either delusions of grandeur with respect to the size of the male organ, and/or an oversexed nature. Such men frequently turn out to be compulsive masturbators.

PEEPING TOM: Frequently indicates someone with a strong sexual appetite and fantasy, who is sexually frustrated and emotionally very private and secretive. Even if such people have a fairly successful relationship, they will nevertheless often be unhappy with their sex life, as they cannot help thinking about the many other people in society who have much richer and more sexually satisfying experiences than they do.

Men who make this doodle are usually strongly attracted to pornographic magazines and films, and erotic literature, though it is possible they may be too embarrassed to admit to this. If, however, such a man's mate is aware of this interest, and has no objection to it, he is bound to make use of such material to stimulate his sexual fantasy in order to relieve any dissatisfaction he may feel with his sex life.

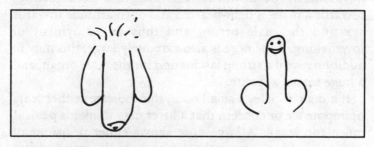

PENIS: If the penis doodled by a woman has a realistic, friendly, or funny-looking appearance, this reveals a keen sense of humour and a flirtatious manner, coupled with abundant sex appeal. This person, without any doubt, thoroughly enjoys socializing with men, and her attitude to sex is very open-minded and light-hearted. Possessing a very sensual nature, and a strong sexual appetite, there is a good chance she will turn out to be a great lover.

If the penis is drawn in an unpleasant or ugly manner, then this reveals very ambiguous feelings towards a woman's lover and/or men and sex in general. Even if she sometimes enjoys lovemaking and feels friendly to her mate, on other occasions she is likely to be filled with resentment and will dislike sex intensely.

If a man habitually doodles the male organ, this shows a

penis fixation coupled with latent bisexual or homosexual tendencies. If the organ is drawn in a very realistic manner, it is likely he feels comfortable with his homosexuality. If, however, the organ is drawn humorously, then it is very possible that he represses this aspect of himself from conscious awareness. If it is drawn in an ugly manner, this often indicates a lack of self-acceptance or even self-hatred, for having such inclinations.

PHALLIC SYMBOLS: Aeroplane, Arrow, Baseball Bat, Car, Chimney, Club, Fishing Rod, Horns on an Animal, Lighthouse, Lobster, Motorbike, Obelisk, Pencil, Pillar, Pole, Rocket, Sceptre, Skyscraper, Spear, Spire or Steeple,

Staff, Tail of an Animal, Tower, Truncheon.

These symbols hint at sexuality that for some reason has no suitable outlet. Consequently, the person concerned is feeling very sexually frustrated and is attempting to escape from such feelings via flights of erotic fantasy. If the phallic symbol that is doodled is broken or has a damaged or weak appearance, this indicates that the person has fears of impotency: indeed, he or she may in reality actually have a weak sex drive or be unable to perform sexually.

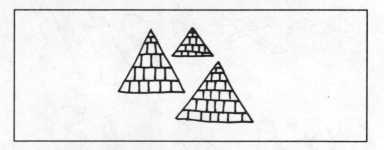

PYRAMID: A female doodler reveals an appreciation of the mystical nature of sex, and a fascination with the mysterious nature of femininity.

A male doodler discloses a sexual nature that fluctuates a great deal. This person's feelings often change from very warm, compassionate and loving, to hostile and intolerant, especially when his sexual needs are denied. This will tend to make his lover feel somewhat confused and insecure in the relationship.

RAINDROPS: If the rain is pictured falling from a dark cloud, this suggests the presence of serious problems in the person's life. Either some serious misfortune has been suffered or, alternatively, there may be an underlying deep dissatisfaction with the person's sex life, and relationships

in general. This doodler will frequently suffer from moods of severe depression.

RIDING DOODLES (whether a horse, or some other animal, or a motorbike or bicycle etc.): See 'Insertion Doodles'.

SAUCEPAN: See 'Cup'.

SAW: See 'Sharp Weapons'.

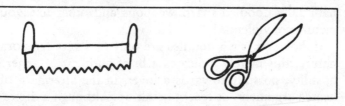

SCISSORS: See 'Sharp Weapons'.

SEASHELL (must be open and deep): See 'Cup'.

SHARP WEAPONS: It is to be hoped that you will not often come across these unpleasant doodles. Someone who habitually draws knives, axes, scalpels, cleavers or any other sharp, weapon-like instruments, is sexually immensely frustrated and repressed. These types, often callous and sadistic, invariably harbour very aggressive feelings towards their mates, and in some cases there may be a general loathing of the opposite sex, possibly stemming from repressed anger and hatred towards a parent-figure. Such people fluctuate between feelings of love and hate, and when gripped by hostile emotions, they are likely to wish terrible harm on others. If their emotional self-control is poor, their partners may be in severe danger of being physically abused in an extremely violent manner. (In some rare cases, the aggression may be turned inwards and then the individual is likely to exhibit extremely self-destructive behaviour and masochistic tendencies possibly even leading to suicide attempts.) Such doodles often appear in drawings of criminals who have been convicted of violent crime, including murder, so if you notice that someone you have just met habitually draws sharp weapons, do not take any chances, just cease contact with him or her altogether. (Denis Nilsen, the English serial killer and cannibal, as well as many other mass murderers, habitually doodled sharp weapons and other unsavoury pictures of violence.)

If, however, such doodles are only of a very temporary nature, this merely indicates a brief outburst of anger or hostility, possibly towards a lover, in the aftermath of a heated argument, or recent break-up. Although a desire to cause injury is still manifested by such doodles, if they are not normally part of the person's doodle repertoire, then the unpleasant thoughts that are producing the violent emotion will usually rapidly fade, and so violent actions are far less likely.

SMILING FACE: Suggests that the person is sexually contented in a satisfying relationship, and likely to approach lovemaking in a light-hearted, open manner.

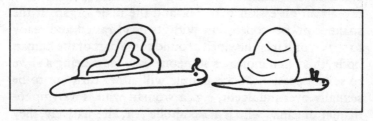

SNAIL: Suggests deep emotional insecurity in the personality. This person is unable to freely express sexual feelings due to strong inhibitions and fear with regard to the act of lovemaking. People who habitually draw this doodle tend to be very secretive, and emotionally repressed, and will carefully hide from their lovers any troubling thoughts and feelings they have about sex. They feel far too embarrassed or ashamed of themselves to speak of such matters. They experience strong feelings of guilt if they masturbate, and if questioned about their thoughts on this subject, may well claim that they do not indulge.

In relationships, they will invariably have a great fear of rivalry, and though they might conceal the fact they are frequently inclined to be gripped by strongly jealous feelings. Such people will be especially attracted to lovers who can offer plenty of protection and security.

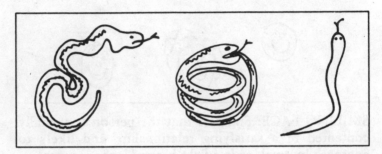

SNAKE: This classic symbol of the phallus undoubtedly reveals an obsession with sex and the male organ. If the snake is drawn coiled, but with its head raised and ready to strike, or if it is entwined around some part of the human body, this often indicates someone who fears being a slave to sexual passions. Such people will either turn out to be sexually over-indulgent, e.g. a woman who is a nymphomaniac or a man who is a 'sexaholic', or, alternatively, they may for some reason be ashamed of their carnal desires and instead develop a sexually repressed and highly frustrated sexual nature. It is not uncommon for women in this category to feel a certain fear or uneasiness at the sight of a fully erect penis.

If the snake is drawn with the tail in its mouth, then this almost certainly represents a deeply passionate and highly erotic, sensual individual who is crazy about sex. Men and women who make this doodle invariably love both giving and receiving oral sex. These types are often aware of the mystical and spiritual connotations of the sexual union, and may well have a deep interest in oriental sexual practices such as those described in the *Kama Sutra* or

Taoist sexual Yoga. Men who make this doodle also invariably have a tremendous confidence in their own virility and their capacity to please a partner.

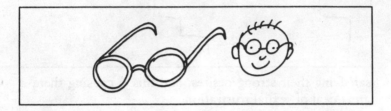

SPECTACLES: Spectacles doodled on to faces in magazines or drawings indicate a humorous but emotionally immature attitude to sex and relationships. These individuals treat foreplay and sexual intercourse in a manner that is likely to be reminiscent of a young teenage adolescent. Although on the surface such a person may give an impression of being at ease, underneath this thin facade hides a human being who is both emotionally and sexually withdrawn, and cannot express openly either sexual desires or heartfelt emotions.

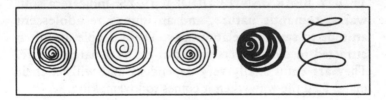

SPIRAL: See 'Snail'.

STAIRS: For people who doodle stairs, sex is an endless fascination and mystery which they have a deep yearning to explore to the full. This picture also reveals that at the moment they are not experiencing much success in

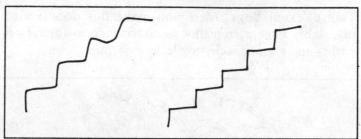

satisfying their strong desires, and this is causing them a great deal of sexual frustration.

SWORD: See 'Sharp Weapons'.

TEDDY BEARS AND CUDDLY TOYS: Indicate a soft, warm, romantic nature, and an immature adolescent attitude to sex and relationships. These people are often attracted to older lovers who can act as a parent-figure. They are emotionally very dependent and will let their mates lead the way when it comes to lovemaking.

TIGER: Represents the enormous power of the human sex drive. People who doodle this animal have, simultaneously, a tremendous respect for and also an underlying fear of the powerful influence exerted on our lives by the fire of sexual desire.

TONGUE: A drawing of a tongue that is poking out of the mouth often discloses a highly sensual individual who thinks constantly about lovemaking. Position 69 is bound to be a favourite with them, as they are absolutely addicted to oral sex. They certainly will not be bashful when explicitly describing to a lover their innermost sexual desires, and when it comes to wildly arousing, erotic sex talk, you can be certain you are dealing with a virtuoso.

TREES: A tree with a round, fluffy, cloud-like crown indicates a friendly, warm-hearted, affectionate nature, a healthy sexual appetite and a strong protective instinct towards a loved one. These types usually have a good sexual fantasy, and with a lover they trust can be very sensual, relaxed and uninhibited in lovemaking.

A bare tree consisting of just branches indicates an emotionally tense and suppressed individual who can be very critical and judgmental towards a lover. In lovemaking these types rarely pay sufficient attention to foreplay, as they are generally overstressed and too impatient.

A full tree with lots of leaves and fruit hanging from the

branches often reveals a warm, sensual, romantic lover who thoroughly enjoys expressing and receiving heartfelt emotion. Such a person will make love in a considerate manner, taking the time necessary to fully enjoy the sensuous delights of erotic kissing and all the other pleasurable components of foreplay.

A tree that has a very sharp, spiky and haphazard appearance signifies immense sexual frustration coupled with a tense and highly irritable nature. This doodle may also be an indication of hostile feelings towards a mate. A love life with this person will rarely be satisfying because this moody nature is not conducive to creating the sort of warm, loving, sensual atmosphere that is needed for a pleasurable sexual union.

A doodle of a Christmas tree drawn in the standard way with sharp, triangular-shaped branches discloses an energetic individual with a fairly strong sex drive. Unfortunately, though, these types are highly rigid in their thinking and have inflexible opinions with regard to how one should behave both in the bedroom and outside it.

Consequently, they have very fixed ideas about sex which makes their manner of lovemaking monotonous, routine, and therefore very predictable and unexciting within the context of a long-term relationship.

A tree that is shaded in a manner that creates a very dark or black impression is a sign of a troubled love life. This may stem from a recent break-up, or alternatively there may be a great deal of emotional and sexual disharmony in the relationship at present. The individual currently feels inadequate, anxious and very worried, and is also inclined to moods of dark depression.

TRIANGLES: Suggests strong sexual appetites that are finding insufficient outlet. In relationships this person is liable to become extremely critical of a mate who fails to satisfy him or her sexually.

UNHAPPY FACE: Regularly doodled, this signifies sexual frustration and a relationship that is filled with conflict. The doodler needs to seek the services of a professional relationship counsellor.

VASE: See 'Cup'.

VEGETABLES: See 'Food'.

VIOLENT SCENES: Almost exclusively drawn by men, any doodles of scenes depicting extreme violence are danger signals that should not be ignored. If you notice that someone habitually produces such gory pictures, then you should steer well clear of them. These types are invariably sexually and emotionally inexperienced and retarded, and immensely frustrated, and their minds are constantly filled with violent fantasies. Such doodles are often drawn by sadistic criminals who have been convicted for violent crime, and even murder.

Read the information given under 'Sharp Weapons' as all of it also applies here.

WEAPONS: See 'Sharp Weapons'.

WHIP: Indicates sexual frustration and, usually, a very cruel streak in the personality, coupled with a fascination for pain and a desire to either inflict or receive punishment. In an intimate relationship, this combination of characteristics will express itself in either sadistic or masochistic behaviour, or more rarely in sadomasochism. Such conduct is likely to affect all areas of the relationship including sex, where the manner of lovemaking will probably have a very violent flavour.

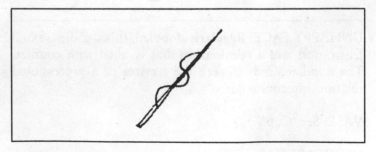

PART THREE

Factors that Seriously Affect the Quality of Sex Life

7. 'Foreplay? Who Cares?'

(SIGNS OF POOR FOREPLAY)

Signs to look for: Handwriting of any style that satisfies one of these points:

1. Writing in which the small letter 't' is consistently made with the crossbar on the right, detached from the stem.

at **hot** get hit- but too

2. Writing in which the small letter 'g' is consistently made with only a descending line. This descending line must be longer than the height of the central zone. (If it is shorter than this, you should refer instead to 'The Occasional Lover', page 256.)

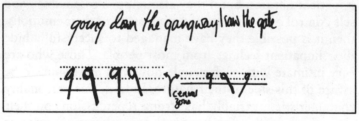

3. Writing in which the small letter 'g' is consistently written like the small letter 'q'.

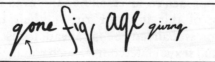

(For information on other behaviour patterns affecting relationship connected with this graphological character-istic, look up these letter-shapes in the relevant part of Part One 'The Alphabet of Sex and Relationship'.)

There are several different graphological signs which can potentially disclose someone who pays insufficient attention to foreplay. The reasons for neglecting this important sensual prelude, however, differ depending upon the particular graphological characteristic seen in the writing. You have therefore been provided with a separate description of the sexual personality associated with each of these graphological indicators. If the writing has two different indicators of this trait, the descriptions of personality connected with both those graphological indicators will apply to the person concerned.

**This first description of sexual behaviour applies
if Point 1 is seen in the writing:**

People with this graphological sign have stressful and impatient natures, but if they also happen to possess good self-control over the outward expression of their emotions, then it is possible they have managed to successfully hide their impatient feelings from most people. Those who are very intimate with such people however, are bound to be aware of this side of their nature. Indeed, this personality characteristic invariably has strong repercussions on their general approach to existence, and most certainly on their sexual behaviour.

Men with this trait are inclined to be very goal-oriented in their approach to lovemaking, and even from the very beginning of this intimate ritual, their thoughts and imagination will already be far ahead, focused on the final stages of full sexual intercourse. Such a man will invariably avoid taking the necessary time to slowly explore his lover's body, and will therefore fail to treat her erogenous zones with the sort of sensitive, loving attention so necessary to achieving a peak level of pleasurable arousal.

These men tend to regard foreplay as being of very secondary importance, a process they are obliged to go through in order to achieve the real end, which is penetration. So whenever they make love they invariably rush through the stages of foreplay, often in the same monotonous, routine manner each time. Their mates are therefore bound to be left feeling very dissatisfied and frustrated, even if they happen to pretend otherwise.

Such men desperately need to learn how to unify their minds with their bodies during the whole process of lovemaking. If they do not, they will never have any chance of increasing their sexual awareness to the point where they understand the very special importance of all those wonderfully stimulating aspects of foreplay that are a prerequisite to a satisfying, healthy and harmonious sexual relationship.

Women with this graphological characteristic do not have such a stereotyped reaction to sex, as their behaviour will be very much influenced by their life style. If a woman with this sign in her writing is very career-oriented, then she may be inclined to view sex as something to get over and done with as quickly as possible, so that she can focus her mind on 'more important matters'.

A woman of this nature, like her male counterpart, is unlikely to put much effort into stimulating her partner with caring foreplay. Equally, there is a fair chance that she will not be particularly concerned, whether or not he devotes sufficient time to her, with such sensual preludes. Indeed, some women with this graphological characteristic even prefer it when their mates virtually avoid this area altogether, jumping ahead instead to full intercourse, so that they can finish lovemaking as quickly as possible. Alternatively, such a woman may just avoid sex altogether, claiming that she has too many other things on her mind.

Very occasionally one comes across women with this graphological sign who do not exhibit the sexual behaviour pattern just described. If they have this indicator in their writing, as well as the graphological indicators of a strong sexual appetite (see 'What's the Score in Bed?' page 303, to determine this) then their sexual manner is likely to be different.

Such an individual may thoroughly enjoy foreplay, and instead of hurrying this area will express the 'speedy' tendencies in her nature via a desire for sudden, unplanned, spontaneous lovemaking sessions that take place in unpredictable places at unexpected times (this is assuming she does not show any obvious signs in her writing of characteristics such as sexual inhibition, which would clearly block the expression of these tendencies).

This second description of sexual behaviour applies if Point 2 is seen in the writing:

Many people with this graphological characteristic have a distinctly ascetic side to their nature that allows them, whenever they wish, to successfully control their basic instincts and desires and detach themselves from their sex drive. They are therefore quite capable of denying themselves sexual and sensual pleasures, as well as other enjoyments in life, for the sake of personal ambition.

Lacking in sensuality and emotional warmth, they will not be particularly imaginative or inspiring when it comes to sex, and this situation cannot be expected to change, unless they choose to place a little less value on matters concerning daily survival, and a little more value on relationship and sensual enjoyments.

This type of 'g' frequently appears in the writing of a man who spends so much time and energy on his career that he often has insufficient vitality left for sex, and consequently loses interest in maintaining the quality of his sexual experiences. Little, if any, attention is paid to the niceties of courtship or foreplay, as his sex life has been reduced to a level where he derives only a very small portion of the pleasure potentially available from lovemaking.

For this individual sex has become only a very mediocre pleasure that merely provides a routine release from the pressures and stress of work. Lacking any real sexual imagination, he will invariably pay little genuine attention to the sexual and sensual needs of his partner, and his robot-like, monotonous sexual antics will often be desperately unexciting. His mate will be left feeling not only dissatisfied, but also somewhat unloved and frustrated, unless he realizes his problem and makes dramatic efforts to deal with it.

A woman with this graphological sign is also unlikely to give sex a high position on her list of priorities, and her partner is bound to consider her an unexciting or even very boring partner, and will inevitably feel very frustrated with her lack of warmth and sensuality (unless of course he happens to have the same sexual nature). Tending to have a very matter-of-fact, unemotional attitude towards sex, this woman will derive little, if any, pleasure from it, and there is a good chance that a stimulating conversation or a good book will be enjoyed significantly more than lovemaking. She will instigate sex only when she feels like it (which will be rarely) and you can be fairly certain that she will not be the sexually passive sort who will give in to the lustful advances of a partner if she herself is not in the mood for sex.

Such women are invariably unresponsive during lovemaking, and they fail to tune into the sexual and sensual needs and desires of their partners. In addition, they are not sexually open-minded, for they almost always have strong opinions about what is, or is not, appropriate sexual behaviour, and will therefore definitely not agree to take part in any unusual or 'way-out' practices. They frequently sublimate their sexual energies into other areas of life such as career and/or family, and this explains, at least partly, their significantly reduced interest in, or need for, sex.

Another possibility with both men and women who show this characteristic is that they possess a negative attitude towards sex that stems from early childhood conditioning by misguided adults. This faulty 'programming' has caused them to block any awareness of pleasant sexual sensations that might be experienced, making lovemaking completely uninspiring and devoid of pleasure and as a consequence of this they do not have much enthusiasm or passion for this area of life.

**This third description of sexual behaviour
applies if Point 3 is seen in the writing:**

People whose writing shows this sign have an exaggerated concern with efficient survival, and this makes it incredibly difficult for them to unwind and relax. This constant inner tension inhibits them from expressing the warmth, sensuality and sexual openness that is so necessary for a gratifying sex life.

If this graphological characteristic shows up in the writing of a woman who leads a highly active existence, then you can be pretty certain that sex will very much take the back-seat in her life. Only very rarely will she seem to find the time for lovemaking, and thus her partner will be left feeling somewhat neglected as well as sexually deprived.

If a man with a busy life style has this writing characteristic, even if he turns out to be the sort who likes to make love regularly, he will nevertheless only tend to enjoy sex as merely a brief, genitally-based release from tension, rather than as a deeply emotional, 'whole body' sensual experience.

Indeed, a sex life with anyone who uses this sign, whether male or female, will probably be very unfulfilling (even if the person happens to have a strong sex drive) because such individuals possess a natural instinct for finding short cuts in whatever they do. Unfortunately however, this useful skill is so ingrained in their personality that it is likely to affect even their sexual behaviour. In lovemaking, therefore, there is a strong likelihood that this person might treat foreplay as an unessential detail, that one can by-pass in order to get to the 'crux of the matter'.

These types often seem to consider it unimportant to take the necessary time to sexually arouse their mates with warm, loving caresses, passionate kisses and erotic massage. Instead, they will invariably take a short-cut and dive headlong into full genital intercourse without any prelude. Until they learn to slow down and take their time during the whole lovemaking process, they will never be able to enjoy the fruits of a fully satisfying intimate relationship.

8. 'This Has Never Happened To Me Before!'

(SIGNS OF SEXUAL IMPOTENCE)

Signs to look for: Handwriting of **any style** that satisfies one or more of these points:

1. Writing of any style in which the pen pressure used on the lower stems of the letter 'g' is almost always noticeably lighter in appearance than the pressure used in the central or upper areas of the writing, e.g. the vowel area and the area occupied by upper stems. (The pen pressure on other lower stems in the writing will, invariably, also be lighter.)

> *going along the gangway*

2. Writing in which the pen pressure used on the lower stems of the letter 'g' varies considerably from heavy to very light. (The same changing pressure pattern will invariably also affect other lower stems in the writing.)

> *are you going to go along again?*

3. Writing in which the stem of the letter 'g' is broken in one or more places (you need to find several examples of this type of 'g').

4. Writing in which the stem of the letter 'g' has a 'wobbly' or shaky appearance (you need to find several examples of this type of 'g').

5. Writing in which the stem of the letter 'g' is always retraced (the upstroke traces over the downstroke).

6. Writing in which the stem of the letter 'g' is consistently so short that it barely descends below the level of the baseline.

Psychologists and therapists specializing in the area of sexual impotence have observed that the etiology of this problem is rarely hormonal or physical in nature. Instead, it appears that emotional conflicts play a far more important role. For instance, it seems that many impotent lovers have enormous difficulty in experiencing feelings of affection at the same time as they experience sexual arousal. Consequently, they might be able to 'make it' with a complete stranger they have just met, but will completely switch off sexually if they attempt to have sex with someone they deeply love.

People with the graphological signs of impotence vary enormously in terms of their sexual nature. To begin with, some of these characters have plenty of sexual energy, whereas others have only a very low amount of sexual vitality. Sometimes the trait of impotence is seen in the writing of an individual with an enormous sexual fantasy, and in other cases there might be no sexual imagination whatsoever. Certain individuals suffering from impotency problems are severely repressed, and yet on other occasions one may come across someone sexually open-minded who has these same sexual difficulties. A person completely uninterested in sex, with an ascetic nature devoid of any warmth or sensuality may well suffer from the same sexual dysfunction as an extremely sensual, tactile human being who is full of genuine desire for lovemaking.

If a reader discovers the signs of impotency in someone's writing, but in addition wishes to determine which of the above sexual categories applies to the person concerned, they will need to carefully read various other chapters in this book.

It should also be remembered that impotency problems vary from one person to another, depending upon an interaction of the above-mentioned factors in combination with a person's early upbringing and adult sexual experiences. It is therefore not possible to know merely from the handwriting which particular sexual dysfunction an individual is suffering from.

The following list, however, covers the main types of impotency problems that may potentially afflict an individual whose writing contains any of the graphological indicators listed above.

In women these may include one or more of the following:

Dispareunia: the woman experiences significant pain during intercourse.

Vaginismus: the vagina is subject to involuntary contractions that can make penetration extremely difficult or even impossible.

Situational Orgasmic Dysfunction: the woman is unable to have orgasms in particular situations. For example, she may climax easily during a brief encounter with a complete stranger whom she knows she will never see again, but cannot reach an orgasm at home with a long-term partner.

Primary Orgasmic Dysfunction: the woman concerned has never had any orgasm whatsoever.

In men, the most common sexual dysfunctions are:

Premature Ejaculation: orgasm is reached so quickly that a partner has no chance of also reaching a climax.

Retarded Ejaculation: the man can maintain his erection, but finds it very difficult, or even impossible to ejaculate during intercourse.

Erectile Dysfunction: there is an inability to have an erection, or alternatively, the erection can be achieved, but not maintained sufficiently long to allow for ejaculation.

Situational Orgasmic Dysfunction: the man is unable to achieve, or alternatively maintain, an erection in particular situations. For example, he may function perfectly adequately with a stranger but cannot perform with his partner.

Many people with quite normal sexual behaviour patterns occasionally suffer from temporary sexual dysfunctions that may stem from a period of unusual stress, tiredness or perhaps a session of excessive drinking. In the case of individuals with the graphological signs of impotence, however, if there is a sexual dysfunction it can often continue for an extended period.

The genesis of any particular person's sexual problems is often difficult to determine. If, however, someone's writing has the graphological characteristic of Point 5 above, any difficulties they are experiencing are likely to result from ideas about sex instilled in them in childhood by their parents, or other adults. (See 'I Could Never Do This With My Partner!', page 196, for a complete description of the sexual nature and etiology of the problems associated with this graphological characteristic.) Writing revealing the graphic features of Points 3 and/or 4 and/or 6 may well indicate factors of physical or psychological ill-health that are responsible for any sexual problems a person may have. If the writing shows the feature described in Point 6, you may also refer to 'The Occasional Lover', page 256 for a complete description of other personality factors associated with this trait.

In other individuals, problems of impotency may occasionally result from hidden insecurities concerning their own heterosexuality. (Check the writing against the graphological signs contained in 'I Wonder...Straight or Gay?', page 205, to see if this may be an influencing factor.) In even more rare instances, if the sexual dysfunction combines with strong fears of physical contact, it may be possible to trace the cause back to an experience of rape or some other frightening or degrading form of sexual abuse that occurred during childhood or early teenage years. Such traumatic events can occasionally be blocked out from the memory, and the person concerned may have no conscious recall of the incident until it perhaps emerges during a course of psychotherapy.

Most problems of impotency, however, can often be best explained by the observation made by the sex researchers

William Masters and Virginia Johnson, who stated, 'fear of inadequacy is the greatest known deterrent to effective sexual functioning, simply because it so completely distracts the fearful individual from his or her natural responsivity by blocking reception of sexual stimuli...'

Anyone suffering from problems associated with impotency should seek help from a therapist specializing in this area as with the right professional guidance many such difficulties can be successfully treated, and a handicap that would otherwise seriously damage relationships can thus be permanently eliminated.

If the graphological indicators of impotency provided in this chapter are present in someone's writing but are not a regular feature of their normal style, then this suggests that any sexual problems they are experiencing are likely to be only very short-lived. They may simply be suffering from a brief onslaught of stress stemming from overwork, lack of sleep, or illness and its after-effects. If this is the case, then this whole description of personality will merely be a temporary state of affairs that will end as soon as they recover from this unusual period of stress.

9. 'I Could Never Do This With My Partner!'

(SIGNS OF SEXUAL REPRESSION)

Signs to look for: Handwriting of any style that satisfies one of the following points:

1. Writing in which the letter 'g' consistently has a stem with an extremely narrow loop.

going giving gaining guiding

2. Writing in which the letter 'g' consistently has a retraced stem (e.g. the upstroke of the pen retraces the downstroke).

gong giggle angling gag

Sigmund Freud once stated that if sex were not considered so 'naughty' it would not be anywhere near as much fun. Many sex therapists agree with this, and realize that it is our inhibitions towards sex that make us view it in this manner. It would seem, therefore, in spite of the current trend towards being completely relaxed and open-minded about sexual activity, that in fact a certain amount of inhibition may actually be a positive stimulus that enhances arousal and excitement.

In people with the graphological characteristics of repression, however, the level of sexual inhibition is excessive, as they are very repressed both emotionally and sexually, and this diminishes enormously the quality of their love life. This problem is clearly a very serious one, as it negatively affects not only their approach to sex, but also many other areas of their existence.

Many leaders within the field of psychotherapy believe repression is a major cause of both mental and physical ill-health. Over the past decade, research within the field of psychosomatic medicine has revealed that people with highly repressed emotional natures tend to internally channel their emotional responses to painful life events. This maladapted reaction upsets the body's hormonal balance and immune system.

Statistics suggest that such individuals are significantly more prone to certain illnesses, including cancer, than those who openly express their emotions. (It is interesting to note that amongst the population of American Sioux Indians, who are renowned for giving free vent to their feelings, there is virtually no incidence of cancer.)

The repressed, sexually inhibited personality is invariably rooted in a pronounced inferiority complex, and suppressed sexual feelings originating from early childhood. This emotionally disturbed condition signals the presence of moral conflict or guilt in attitudes towards sexual arousal. At some time during their childhood years, such people developed the erroneous idea that sexual excitement and the desire it stimulated is dirty or sinful in some way. They anxiously struggled to keep their sexual feelings under tight control and were consumed by guilt whenever they succumbed to the sensual pleasures of self-stimulation.

Locked away for so many years in the darkest recesses of the subconscious, these fermenting, festering desires have provided a comfortable soil for the roots of these people's current sexual neuroses. The resulting nervous tension and low self-esteem has created a vicious circle, feeding the energy of sexual suppression and increasing even further the fear of letting go. Their emotions are bottled up tightly, and they are being slowly eaten away inside by their desperately inhibited feelings with regard to sex. This intense fear and insecurity may not be evident to others, as such people hide themselves behind a wall of secrecy. They develop rigid, routine patterns of thinking and behaving in order to construct and support a well-defined framework for their existence. This allows them to feel more in control of their lives, and therefore helps to reduce the underlying anxiety they have of not being able to cope adequately with the demands of existence.

Unfortunately, however, this familiar, safe little world they have created has simultaneously become a self-made prison; by remaining within its walls they are blocking inner growth and destroying any hope of breaking free from the shackles of their severely repressed inhibited feelings.

Being very judgmental in their attitude to others, they will inevitably be exceptionally careful in their choice of mate. In relationships, a compulsive adherence to routine and lack of any easy-going spontaneity tends to make them irritatingly predictable (especially in the area of sex) and they are liable to be very tiring and tedious at times. They always like to know in advance exactly what they are going to be doing and what is expected of them, in order to carefully and cautiously plan and prepare their movements.

Inwardly critical and wary of people, and possessing an unusually private, secretive nature, these types are usually ultra-cautious of others, and even those intimate with them are unlikely ever to come close to the inner sanctuary of their hidden thoughts and feelings. Socially, many such individuals adopt a rather over-formal or aloof manner, and being highly selective will shy away from expanding their circle of friends, preferring to limit themselves to one or possibly two close companions. If they are in a relationship with someone who is highly gregarious and enjoys being surrounded by hordes of people, this will definitely be a potential area of conflict between them.

A love-life with such a person will inevitably be fraught with problems, due to the tight rein kept over sensual appetites and instinctive urges.

These types invariably feel very uneasy about nudity, so at the start of a new relationship they may well try to hide their nakedness from a lover by undressing in the dark or keeping underwear on until they are beneath the sheets. Many people with this characteristic experience great discomfort and embarrassment if they have to make love with the light on. They are far too inhibited to talk freely about sexual matters, because they fear that a disclosure of these thoughts and feelings would lead to their being rejected. Consequently, it will be almost impossible for them to discuss their own or their partner's sexual needs. Any erotic thoughts they have will certainly be kept private. Even in a very close relationship, no one is likely to know much about their feelings and desires in the area of sex. Consequently, their manner of lovemaking will probably be very unimaginative, conventional and highly predictable, and lacking in warmth, sensuality and passion.

Sometimes the graphological signs of sexual inhibition can appear in the handwriting of so-called 'sexually liberated' men and women. Very often, such individuals are capable of candidly explaining to their partners exactly what they want sexually, and their outer behaviour may indeed be truly liberated, but in spite of this they are still deeply affected by their sexual inhibitions. Whilst the conscious part of their brain is telling them that everything they are doing and saying is perfectly all right and that they should go ahead and enjoy themselves, underneath all this the subconscious level of their mind is trying to hold them back. The conflict between these two levels of awareness significantly reduces the pleasure they gain from their apparently 'liberated' lovemaking.

Others with this graphological characteristic (usually women) may avoid initiating any type of sexual advance whatsoever. They seem to believe that they do not really have any sexual needs, and appear genuinely not to be interested in such matters. If such a woman's partner is aroused, she may be willing to have sex with him, out of love or 'duty', but she will not be prepared to admit to herself that she is doing this for any other reason. These women can derive pleasure from sex, free of any anxiety and guilt, only if they can convince themselves that the matter is out of their control; that they are not responsible for their sexual actions because they have been forced into them.

Occasionally, one comes across people with this graphological sign who are so wary of lovemaking that they use subtle 'sex-avoidance' tactics: for instance, a man may habitually become involved with some late-night movie. Later on, his partner will probably be too exhausted for any 'action' and just want to sleep; if not, he will use the perfectly reasonable and acceptable excuse that he himself is simply too tired to make love.

Another common behaviour pattern with sexually inhibited people is revealed by those who thoroughly enjoy making love with someone, and then when it is over they are overwhelmed by feelings of guilt, anxiety and also regret. Again, as with all the other examples of sexually inhibited behaviour mentioned previously, this is a product of sexual hang-ups formed during childhood.

Some men with sexual inhibitions seem to lose them if they can have sex with someone outside their regular relationship. A man of this type is often too embarrassed to reveal his innermost erotic desires to his partner, because he feels his mate is too 'nice' or 'innocent' to be subjected to such 'carnal passion'. Alternatively, he may simply believe that his sexual cravings will be considered 'unclean' or perverted in some way, and he fears being despised and rejected if he attempts to express them. Consequently, he will rarely be turned on by his mate, and his standard of lovemaking will probably be very poor.

During an act of infidelity though, such men can drop their inhibitions and perform well. Under these circumstances, they feel perfectly comfortable to really enjoy themselves, indulging their wildest erotic fantasies (that are usually suppressed) with this 'forbidden' female, without any fear of being rejected for having 'filthy' needs. Invariably, the woman chosen for this purpose will be someone whom they consider loose or immoral, as only then can they freely express their erotic urges without any fear of being negatively judged.

Unfortunately it often happens that when a man lives with a woman who has sexual inhibitions, he may well make the serious mistake of misinterpreting her unwillingness to satisfy his sexual needs as a sign that she does not really love him enough. Often the attitude will be, 'any woman who really loved me would do this thing for me'. This, however, is an entirely false assumption, as the woman concerned may in fact love him very deeply, and still be absolutely incapable of showing this in the manner that he believes she should.

It would seem clear from all this, that if one or both partners in a relationship is sexually very inhibited, then the quality of their lovemaking is likely to be seriously impaired. Fortunately, however, there are many simple ways in which sexually inhibited men and women can overcome their fears, and books written offering information on this subject can sometimes be very helpful. If, however, the inhibitions are very pronounced, then the person concerned should definitely seek the help of a professional therapist who is experienced with such problems.

If the lower stems on the letter 'g' are predominantly retraced, i.e. the upstroke retraces the downstroke (see Point 2 on page 196), in addition to all the information above, the following also applies:

People with this writing characteristic have a perfectionist streak, and will strive for exactness, precision and error-free performance in everything they do. Such retraced stems also frequently reveal obsessive compulsive behaviour patterns, and often these people will have a tendency to compulsively double-check everything, out of fear that something may have been forgotten. For example, someone might carefully lock the front door when leaving home, and then a short while later become fixated on the idea that perhaps a mistake was made and the door did not in fact lock correctly. This obsessive streak is liable to affect other areas of behaviour, and anyone living with such people is liable to find them at times excessively fussy and pedantic.

As a defence from feeling, it is not uncommon for such individuals to just switch off sexually, and they will often do the same with their other emotions. Consequently, they are likely to appear cold and aloof to a partner, when the reality is that they are simply terrified of acknowledging their emotions. When these types make love, they do not allow themselves to become deeply involved, but instead almost always seem to stand outside of themselves, adopting a spectator role during the whole act. Undue attention is focused upon performance, and fears about sexual competence frequently predominate. There may, in some cases, also be a general sense of disapproval or disgust with the whole process of lovemaking. The devastating effect that this will have on the quality of such a person's sex life hardly needs stating.

Inhibited people live in dread of what might be released if they lost control over their instinctual desires, and in some cases these severe inhibitions towards sex can cause sexual impotency. (For a list of the most common dysfunctions of sexual impotence that one is most likely to come across, see 'This Has Never Happened To Me Before!', page 193.)

This impotency may be merely temporary, but in the case of individuals with the graphological signs of severe repression it can often continue for some time.

These sexual problems inevitably stem from unhealthy or warped ideas about sex, instilled in those affected by misguided parents, or other adult figures who had influence over them during their early childhood years. In some cases, an excessively puritanical religious background that denigrated sexual enjoyment may have been the cause. This negative programming precipitated a perception of sexual activity as something dirty or sinful that should be controlled and suppressed. The experience of sexual arousal and the lustful desires it stimulated would have been accompanied by considerable anxiety and guilt, and exaggerated feelings of self-disgust were undoubtedly felt whenever they indulged in masturbation. They may also have developed insecurities concerning their own heterosexuality. In some instances, the genesis of severe sexual repression or fear of sexual contact in people with this graphological sign may be traced back to some childhood sexual experience that has been blocked from the memory.

If someone with writing containing a predominance of retraced stems suffers from any of the above-mentioned problems, then professional help should be sought from a therapist specializing in sexual problems. With the right guidance, such people should be able to gradually develop a wholesome and uncritical acceptance of their own and their partners' sexuality, which will lead to unimpeded enjoyment of sexual arousal, culminating naturally in a fully satisfying orgasmic experience.

When physical and emotional repression remains unresolved, sexual energy in the body is forced to find other routes of escape, perhaps via inordinately long working hours or excessive sporting activity. If, however, release is not provided, then it is very probable that there will be an extreme build-up of pressure that is unleashed in a destructive manner. Such individuals are likely to suffer from damagingly high levels of nervous tension, and may exhibit hostile or exaggeratedly authoritarian attitudes to their partners, possibly to defend their already poor self-esteem from questions or criticism. Other anti-social and perhaps reclusive tendencies may also develop.

10. 'I Wonder...
Straight or Gay?'

(SIGNS OF HOMOSEXUALITY)

GROUP A (MAJOR SIGNS)

Possible homosexual tendencies can be surmised from a writing sample if it satisfies at least one of the following four points:

1. Several examples of the small letter 'g' or 'y' with a balloon-shaped stem of any shape that is very noticeably extended to the left.

2. Several examples of the small letter 'g', 'j', 'y', 'f' or 'q' with a double-looped stem that looks like a number eight. (Note how the ascending line rises up first, on the right-hand side of the descending line, prior to moving to the left and back again to the right to form the double loop.)

3. Several examples of the capital letter 'J' with a balloon-shaped stem of any shape that is very noticeably extended to the left.

4. Several examples of capital or small letters with any type of phallus-shaped appearance or protrusion.

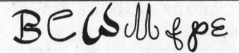

GROUP B (MINOR SIGNS)

Possible homosexual tendencies can be surmised from a writing sample if it satisfies at least three of the following thirteen points:

1. Writing with one or more of the following four characteristics:

• Writing containing many letters clogged with ink.

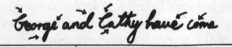

• Writing with a muddy, smudgy, or smeary appearance.

- Writing done from choice with a thick felt-tip pen, or any other pen producing broad, thick lines.

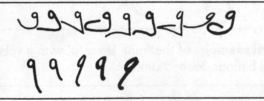

- Writing in which heavy pen pressure makes indentations that clearly show on the reverse of the paper.

2. Writing with several examples of the small letter 'g' with a stem of any shape that does not form a loop, but which is very noticeably extended to the left, or alternatively, with a lower stem that generally has no ascending line whatsoever, and curves a little to the right.

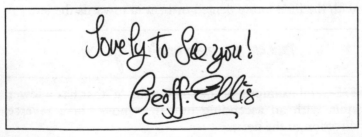

3. Large, flamboyant, round-looking writing with wavy flourishes or extra embellishments and large, ornate capital letters, together with a large, flamboyant, ornate signature with flourishes and extra embellishments.

4. Writing in which the letter 'g' is made with four or more noticeably different formations of stem. (The sample below shows a wide selection of noticeably different stem formations.)

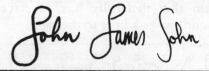

5. Several examples of the capital letter 'J' which is written like a letter 's'.

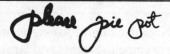

6. Several examples of the small letter 'p' with a very large, rounded balloon-looped stem.

7. Several examples of the small letter 'm' which is written with the final hump dented or bent in towards the left.

8. Several examples of the small letter 'g' that has a lower stem with an ascending line that moves in a reverse direction to the norm.

9. Writing that is strongly left slanted, with many examples of letter 'g' stems that are either a descending line that is generally noticeably thicker at the tip, or alternatively just a very long, dangling, descending line.

10. Several examples of the small letter 'g' with a large, rounded stem containing a large hook at its tip.

11. Male writing that has a feminine appearance containing letters that begin with a rigid diagonal line starting from noticeably below the central zone.

To be classified as feminine, the writing must satisfy the requirements of Points *a.* and *b.* below. If however only one of these two points fits, then the writing must also meet the requirements of Points *c.* and *d.*

a. Almost all the connecting strokes between letters are softly curved rather than straight or angled.

b. Most of the letter formations occupying the central zone of the writing (the vowel area) are softly rounded rather than sharp or angular.

209

c. Many looped upper stems are very rounded at the top.

d. Most of the letter 'i's have a round circle instead of a dot.

it isnt always easy to find

it isnt always easy to find

12. Several examples of the small letter 'x' where the cross is significantly longer on the left side, and sinks well below the baseline.

when extra time starts it gets exciting

13. Several examples of one or more of the following four types of unusual letter formation:

a. Flags on the upper stems of letters; these take the form of small reversed strokes which are high on upper zone stems, and made with a swinging lead-in stroke.

I hope both of you arent leaving too?

b. Capital or small letters with an 'Eagle's Talon' formation.

g g g g g dog arent

c. The reversed 'd' which is written starting from the top of the stem and going downwards.

don't demand do and did and

d. Portions of letters which should be entirely in the central zone, have extensions which sink noticeably below the baseline.

hat dog at are back me no cheat

You are requested to use the information contained in this chapter with the greatest of caution. When the idea for this book first came into being, I made a firm decision not to reveal any graphological signs which potentially disclose homosexuality. I was concerned that in the wrong hands such material might be misinterpreted, or even used in a negative manner. In spite of this earlier decision, I felt it necessary to include this very important chapter on human sexuality, firstly in order to dispel the numerous ambiguous or misleading ideas on the subject that have appeared over recent years in certain other books on graphology, and secondly because a growing number of people today, both in gay circles as well as amongst heterosexuals, have developed an accepting attitude towards homosexuality.

This whole subject has, however, always been a source of great controversy, and is likely to continue to be so for many years in the future. As with all areas of human behaviour, there is much that still needs to be answered before we come to understand fully the various interacting forces of existence that determine the sexual preferences of any individual.

All the cells in the human body possess the characteristics of both sexes, and it is also a biological fact that every human being, irrespective of sex, secretes both male and female hormones – androgens (such as testosterone) and oestrogens respectively. Males however, produce more androgens, whereas females produce more oestrogens. Neither cells nor glands therefore, are at the service exclusively of a single sex.

Freud was convinced that human beings are born with a bisexual potential. He was clearly expressing this belief when he spoke of 'the great enigma of the biological fact of the duality of the sexes'.

Carl Gustav Jung also understood that the human personality is a blend of male and female characteristics. He claimed that every male has a female side to his psyche, and this lives in the unconscious part of the mind. He called this female element the 'anima'. Similarly, females have a male side to their personality called the 'animus', also existing in the unconscious mind. In this sense, Jung was clearly attributing to human beings androgynous or bisexual qualities.

Homosexual activity, and especially bisexual behaviour, seems to have increased significantly over the past few decades. Perhaps the reason for this changing trend is hinted at in a humorous comment made by Woody Allen: 'Bisexuality immediately doubles your chances of a date on Saturday night.'

To apply the above graphological knowledge correctly, it is essential that you keep in mind the following three key points:

1. If you come across the graphological signs of

homosexuality in someone's writing, this merely indicates they have homosexual, or possibly bisexual inclinations. It does not necessarily mean they actually lead a homosexual or bisexual existence.

An individual in this category might, for various reasons, lead an entirely heterosexual life style. Some people with homosexual tendencies choose to suppress them because they fear being rejected by friends, colleagues or even family. In addition, although Aids is a terrible illness which threatens everyone in society, many male homosexuals believe that the risk of contracting this deadly virus is greater if a man chooses a gay or bisexual way of life. Consequently, there are cases of male teenagers, still virgins, who in spite of strong desires for their own sex, choose instead to adopt a completely heterosexual life style, because they fear this increased risk of Aids. This same fear has even occasionally caused a changeover to a purely heterosexual life style in men who, prior to the advent of the Aids virus, may have been involved for many years in homosexual or bisexual relationships.

2. Are the graphological signs of homosexuality given in this chapter very reliable indicators of this characteristic? The answer is yes – if they are seen in someone's writing this definitely shows strong homosexual tendencies. However, as mentioned in Point 1, one cannot know for certain whether the behaviour is actively expressed or merely a latent potential. There is another very important fact that you should always keep in mind when using the information in this book: the fact that someone is gay does not necessarily mean their writing will contain any graphological indicators of homosexuality. This does not reflect a special weakness in the system of handwriting analysis as compared with other methods of personality

assessment, for all the behavioural sciences (psychology, psychiatry, etc.) are prone to the same sort of difficulty. Some gay people reveal their sexual preferences very clearly via facial and other body gestures, whereas others are absolutely indistinguishable from their heterosexual counterparts. Some gays have a writing style which contains classic graphological signs of homosexuality, and yet others, who are also homosexual, may have no gay signs in their writing whatsoever. Frequently, writing in this second category belongs to individuals who have no hang-ups about their sexual preferences. They feel completely at ease, and fulfilled with their sexuality.

3. Four graphological signs are listed in this chapter under the heading Group A (Major Signs). These are such strong indicators of homosexuality that even if they are seen on their own in the writing, in the absence of any other indicators one can deduce the possibility that there may be homosexual inclinations in the personality.

The rest of the signs that appear in this chapter however, under the heading Group B (Minor Signs) mean absolutely nothing if seen without other supporting signs. You have to see at least three of these in combination in order to detect the possible presence of gay tendencies. On no account whatsoever should you interpret possible homosexual or bisexual inclinations on the basis of just one or two of the graphological signs in the Group B section.

FAMOUS GAYS

(signature)	Tchaikovsky
(signature)	Liberace
(signature)	James Dean
(signature)	Michelangelo
(signature)	Martina Navratilova

11. 'Are You In Danger?'

(SIGNS OF VIOLENCE)

GROUP A

Signs to look for: Handwriting of **any style** that satisfies one or more of the following six points:

1. Writing which has an extremely muddy, smudgy, or smeary appearance.

> *walking along the road*
> *this is very difficult to do*

2. Writing where the pen pressure is generally so great that it tears holes in the paper in various places.

3. Writing produced almost exclusively by zig-zag movements of the pen, so that the appearance is extremely jagged. The pressure of the writing must also be heavy enough so that one can see the indentations on the reverse of the paper. (This sign does not apply to calligraphic writing styles such as italics.)

> *I am coming home now*

4. Writing containing capital or small letters with a blunt, club-shaped part.

A E G got and at are

5. Writing in which the letters 'a' or 'o', as well as other letters, are split into two or more disconnected parts.

abcdefghmnvsye

6. Writing with many examples of letters clogged with ink seen in combination with one or more of the following signs listed below:

George and Cathy have come

- 'The Whip' – capital or small letters with a final line that rises noticeably higher and curves or 'whips' to the right (look out for this sign on the capital letters 'H', 'V' and 'W', or the small letters 'v' or 'w'). For detailed information on the meaning of this sign, see Chapter 2, 'Key Symbols', page 44.

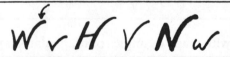

- 'The Jagged Tower' – capital or small letters that begin with a sharply angled peak rising noticeably above the rest of the letter (look out for this sign particularly on the capital letters 'B', 'M' and 'R', or the small letters 'b', 'h' or 'm'). For detailed information on the meaning of this sign, see Chapter 2, 'Key Symbols', page 55.

M hat B met

- 'The Sharp Knife' – capital or small letters containing a razor-sharp, knife-like formation. For detailed information on the meaning of this sign, see Chapter 2, 'Key Symbols', page 67.

D C S g h f y

- Writing in which the small letters 'h', 'm' and 'n' are nearly always sharply angled at the top and bottom.

mahogany HUMAN

- Sharply pointed loops on upper and lower stems.

together forever and always

- Writing with many examples of triangular-shaped stems.

I agree you should go away

• Writing with several examples of the small letter 't' with the crossbar sloping noticeably downwards.

but date but hit cat sit

GROUP B

Signs to look for: Handwriting of any style that satisfies Points 1 or 2, as well as one or more of the other points listed below:

1. Writing with many examples of letters clogged with ink seen in combination with one or more of the following signs listed below.

2. Writing of such heavy pressure that indentations can be clearly seen on the reverse side of the paper.

3. Writing with an extremely uncontrolled, restless appearance (inconsistency in areas such as size and slope of writing and alignment as well as any other features that give the writing this appearance).

feel so inwardly restless

4. Several examples of the small letter 'd' that lean to the right noticeably more than the rest of the writing (you must see two or more 'd's that do this).

intended collected found

5. Writing with many examples of letters that have been written over, as well as several examples of words that have been heavily crossed out.

6. Several examples of 'd's with a looped stem that is at least twice as wide as the central zone.

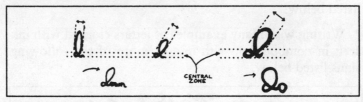

7. Writing in which some of the words are printed in capitals and some in cursive script.

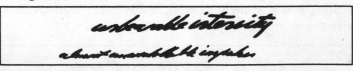

8. Writing which leans so far to the right that it looks as if it might fall over.

9. Very uneven pressure in the writing. This is revealed by sudden increases in pressure appearing as darkening of some words or parts of words.

Anyone who enters into a relationship with someone whose writing fits the description of Group A and/or Group B in this chapter runs a very definite risk of becoming a victim of physical violence.

These graphological signs are usually indicative of physically violent behaviour. It should be noted, however, that women with these handwriting characteristics are unlikely to exhibit nearly as much violent behaviour as men with the same signs. This is partly due to the fact that in almost all cultures on this earth, females are 'programmed' to believe that the physical expression of aggression is unacceptable and unfeminine. In the male population, however, such hostile behaviour is far more tolerated, and sometimes even encouraged, as an expression of manliness.

There is also a physiological reason for this difference, which perhaps carries even more weight. Scientists from various disciplines researching the biological basis of behaviour have come up with conclusive evidence that the quantity of the hormone testosterone in the body strongly influences not only the sex drive but also the level of aggression, in humans as well as in other animal species.

Higher levels of testosterone tend to correlate closely with stronger sexual urges and an increase in the expression of belligerent or hostile behaviour. In the human species, this hormone is twenty times higher in men than in women. Consequently, a man with graphological characteristics that suggest violence in the personality will be far more prone to expressing anger in a physically violent manner than a woman with the same writing trait.

GROUP A

People with writing that contains any of the points listed in this group feel a compulsive desire to control others and when they choose they are capable of using their highly aggressive temperament to rapidly intimidate weaker beings into submission. If their wishes are not gratified, they can become extremely angry, and they will always attempt to even the score if someone crosses them.

Individuals with such tendencies are often the victims of an overly oppressive childhood, controlled by a domineering parent-figure who may have subjected them to severe psychological and/or physical punishment. This badly damaged their self-esteem and created frustrated, angry feelings, that under certain circumstances are released via physically aggressive outbursts of anger.

In relationships, this person will be an absolute tyrant, and when angry will point out faults in a partner's personality in order to destroy self-confidence and humiliate them.

Men especially with this personality make-up are inclined to settle an argument with violence if they feel they are likely to be on the losing side. If deprived of what he considers to be his 'rights', such a man may use physical violence to compel his partner to satisfy him.

For a full description of people whose writing shows Point 4 in Group A (blunt, club-shaped formations on letters) see 'The Blunt Club' on page 62.

People with writing that contains the signs described in Point 5 in Group A (the letters 'a' or 'o', as well as other letters, are split into two or more disconnected parts) could well turn out to be unbelievably dangerous. These particular signs are likely to betray an extremely disturbed psyche that is capable of committing acts of extreme destruction either to the writer or to others. Such graphological features have been seen in the writing of suicidally inclined drug addicts, as well as the worst of murderers (note the writing of Jeffrey Dahmer, the serial killer and cannibal).

GROUP B

People with writing that satisfies points listed in Group B may in fact be perfectly reasonable, decent human beings. The problem is, however, that when they become very stressed, frightened or frustrated, their anger and tension build up to such a crescendo that they completely lose their emotional and physical self-control and are capable of explosive outbursts of anger that can rapidly lead to physically violent behaviour being unleashed on those they love most, or even on total strangers. In relationships these people tend to have excessive expectations from their loved ones, and if these needs are not met this can easily trigger off aggressive reactions.

This behaviour pattern can often be traced back to a childhood plagued by frequent criticism and/or physical punishment, or alternatively, unhappiness created by conflicts between parents. This damaged the child's self-esteem and created a guilt complex in the personality as well as an intense fear of rejection, and the interaction of these three neurotic characteristics has produced this unbalanced emotional nature.

Such people are invariably over-sensitive to criticism and often even well-meant advice will be considered a put-down. They are clearly very vulnerable to a negative emotional atmosphere, and are unable to tolerate any form of hostile behaviour from others.

Such people should obviously avoid any kind of pressured life style for it is stress, strain and tension which often provoke the loss of psychological equilibrium which leads to their neurotic emotional outbursts.

MEN OF VIOLENCE

Stalin

Jack the Ripper

Mussolini

Himmler

your sincire last letter really got too me —

Al. De Salvo

Albert de Salvo, 'The Boston Strangler'

Reggie Kray

FAILURE TO COMPLY WITH THESE
REQUESTS MEANS - NO ONE WILL EVER
SEE THE GIRL AGAIN. ...
The affair must end one way or
the other within 3 days. 72 HRS.
YOU WILL RECEIVE FURTHER
NOTICE,
But the terms Remain the Same.
FATE
If you want aid against me ask GOD not man

Edward Hickman

Edward Hickman, kidnapper and murderer

reine Wahrheit darstellen Feldmarschall um nochma des ergangenen Urteils.

Josef Kramer

Joseph Kramer, Nazi 'Beast of Belsen' and Kommandant of Auschwitz

Udo von Woyrsch, SS leader of a Nazi extermination squad

Napoleon

MONDAY 8TH FEB. 1993 RONKRAY
BROADMOOR HOSPITAL
PUT YOUR NAME
HIS HOLIDAYS
SOON

Ronnie Kray

12. 'Everybody, Look At Me! Am I Wonderful?'

(SIGNS OF NARCISSISM)

Some of the characteristics of narcissism can be surmised from a writing sample if it satisfies one of the nine points listed in Group A (Major Signs). If a writing sample satisfies two or more of these points or, alternatively, one of these points and two or more of the points in Group B (Minor Signs) you can be fairly certain you are dealing with a classic example of the narcissist personality.

GROUP A (MAJOR SIGNS)

1. Very large writing, that has a central zone as large or larger than this:

2. Any signature that is either extremely large, or large and showy.

3. Capital letters that are generally extremely large and showy.

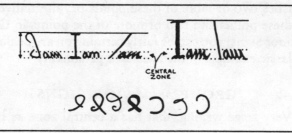

4. Any personal pronoun 'I' that is either very large (at least four times the size of the central zone) or a personal pronoun that contains a large, rounded, balloon-shaped loop, or a large semi-circle that is wide open to the left.

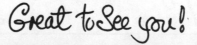

5. Flamboyant, round-looking writing with wavy flourishes and extra embellishments.

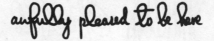

6. Writing in which many of the upper stems of letters have very large, balloon-shaped loops of any shape.

7. Writing with letters containing spiral formations.

8. Writing in which all the letters within words are printed in large, embellished or stylish-looking capitals.

9. The small letter 'd' which has a very over-inflated balloon-shaped stem that crosses over the oval portion of the letter, or alternatively, loops around to enclose the whole of the oval portion.

GROUP B (MINOR SIGNS)

The characteristic of narcissism can also be surmised from a writing sample if it satisfies at least four of the following points:

1. Writing with many examples of the small letter 'm' formed with two loops, giving it the appearance of two small letter 'e's.

2. Writing with many examples of the small letter 'p' with a stem that has a very over-inflated balloon-shaped appearance.

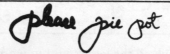

3. Writing with extremely short or stunted-looking upper and lower stems that are 'stick-like' (without loops).

4. Endings on most of the letter 'd's and 't's which descend noticeably below the base of the letter.

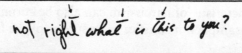

5. The small letter 't' frequently written with the crossbar floating above the stem.

not right what is this to you?

6. Several examples of the small letter 'g' or 'y' with a balloon-shaped stem of any shape that is very noticeably extended to the left. (If you see this sign in the writing, then refer also to 'I Wonder...Straight or Gay?', page 205.)

7. Writing with many examples of tangled loops in oval formations (e.g. tangled 'o's and 'a's, and letters such as 'd' and 'g' where the oval portion of the letter contains tangled loops).

8. Any signature underlined by more than one line or by a single line that is wavy or elaborate.

People with the graphological signs of the narcissist are excessively self-absorbed, and grossly over-concerned and obsessed with the way life is treating them, to the point where the feelings, needs and wishes of those around them are often completely ignored and overwhelmed by the intensity of their own personal desires and ambitions.

They are highly subjective in their perception of others, because their own wishes and needs occupy so much space in their minds that everything else is overshadowed and true perspective is distorted. Indeed, if their desires are thwarted, they are liable to overreact and blow up, out of all proportion, what are merely trivial occurrences.

The main motivating force in their life comes from a relentless desire to gain a position of distinction for themselves. They shine when they are the centre of attention, and invariably have a strong, poised social presence and an entertaining charismatic manner, coupled with a natural sense of showmanship as well as

231

exhibitionist tendencies. This allows them to project a highly credible and impressive image of themselves. In reality, though, this is merely a thin veneer which conceals a highly insecure, disturbed neurotic psyche. These people suffer terribly because they have rejected and lost contact with their true selves and are striving in vain to reconstruct for themselves a new identity based upon an idealistic image of who they think they should be. Their lives are ruled by a thirst for love, admiration and attention, a desperate need to be recognized and accepted as truly exceptional human beings. Image and status are of paramount importance to them, but their restless nature is impossible to satisfy because they want too much out of life.

The characteristic of narcissism is fairly widespread, particularly among the population of the developed countries of the world. This is hardly surprising, when one considers that many cultures today strongly encourage narcissistic behaviour through their attitude towards the rich, successful and famous. The people that society admires most are generally those who have achieved the most prominent or acclaimed positions in the world of politics, entertainment, business or sport. These well-known public personalities are invariably very self-interested individuals who are so caught up in their own ambitions that they have little genuine concern for the problems of the rest of the world, except where they are directly affected.

Narcissists can be extremely charming in order to gain attention and affection, but in spite of this friendly facade they often lack genuine empathy for other people. Even if they are capable of demonstrating sympathy and compassion for others, such feelings are rarely, if ever, long-lasting. Narcissists intent on portraying a successful social image, often seem to relate to the rest of the world as though it is a giant audience that exists in order to provide them with applause and admiration. Other human beings appear to be merely a background to the drama of their existence. In intimate relationships, this behaviour pattern makes it very difficult for them to reach a deep sense of personal connectedness with a partner. Such individuals are rarely capable of expressing the sort of selfless love, and heartfelt altruism, that exists in a genuinely mature and meaningful relationship. Instead, they demonstrate at times an almost childlike egocentricity.

Some narcissists, however, realizing the inappropriateness of such behaviour, manage to camouflage it by acting as though they really care. Socially, many people in this category will present an image to others that is incredibly friendly and charming, but the warmth in many cases is simply a front designed to manipulate others into providing what they want. Indeed, anyone considering a relationship with such a person should remember that the old cliché 'appearances can be deceptive' applies to this character. During the early stages of a relationship, narcissists can be incredibly enthusiastic about their recently found 'love', for they tend to idealize new partners and easily become infatuated with the fantasy image they have created of the person they are with. They are prepared to work very hard to earn the love and admiration of this wonderful human being they desperately need, but unfortunately, once they feel the prize is theirs, there is a very high probability that within a fairly short time they will no longer appreciate their treasure and, becoming restless and bored, they are liable to seek change in the form of new conquests in order to feel good again.

Narcissists find it especially difficult to establish satisfying long-term relationships, and this problem is further exacerbated by their inability to view a partner realistically. Instead of seeing and accepting their mate's true identity, they begin the relationship by idealizing them and end it by devaluing them.

Narcissists are always very demanding, and their desire for status makes them highly critical of any mate they think will not enhance their social image. They expect and require abundant emotional and physical satisfaction from their partners, but once the excitement of a new love has cooled down they themselves give very little back in return. What they do contribute tends to be what they think is best, rather than what is really needed or wanted. Consequently, any lovers they have are likely to feel emotionally rejected and frustrated, as a result of continually having to provide far more than they receive.

When narcissists are living with people who do not make sufficient effort to satisfy their needs, or when things in their lives are not going according to plan, they are inclined to severe mood swings of depression, and may well feel that they have been let down by those who are supposed to help them.

If two narcissists start a relationship together, there is usually a period of exaggerated enthusiasm and infatuation, based upon idealized perceptions of one another that are reinforced by the false social front that each adopts in order to impress. When both parties realize the truth of the situation, either they will decide to accept, and continue with, the empty facade of their relationship, hiding the truth of their mistake from others for the sake of appearances, or the relationship may turn into a battleground where the partners fight for the position of centre stage, while punishing one another for not fulfilling their respective needs.

What causes narcissism? Psychologists have observed

that the complete self-absorption and inner feelings of inadequacy and insecurity typical of the narcissist is a behaviour pattern that is likely to have been with the individual since early childhood, when he or she felt either underprivileged or rejected in some way. This state of mind may stem from emotional deprivation due to insufficient parental affection and attention during crucial formative years, or perhaps the parents had excessive expectations which could not be fulfilled. Alternatively, such a child may have been judged, criticized, or devalued in a manner that resulted in the complete destruction of self-esteem.

Whatever the cause, one thing is certain: beneath the outer behaviour of these individuals hides a little child who feels unloved, unwanted and unimportant. Feelings of loneliness and isolation combine with a sense of self-disgust and in some cases even self-hatred, and it is these confused negative emotions that fuel much of the narcissist's behaviour, making it remarkably difficult for them to genuinely love other people.

Extremely dissatisfied with their own personality, and/or feeling unable to live up to parental demands, narcissists begin in early childhood to create a new image of themselves, designed to be an object of praise and admiration instead of criticism. To achieve this, however, unfortunately required a simultaneous denial and suppression of the true self. This rapidly resulted in a total loss of contact with the authentic side of their personality, which was repressed in their unconscious. It is narcissists' rejection and denial of who they really are that is responsible for their intense inner feelings of emptiness. In their futile efforts to escape this, they unwittingly develop attitudes and behaviour patterns that are counter-productive to their own and other people's happiness and peace of mind. No matter how much love, success and good luck they may have, existence never seems to meet their expectations and they feel constantly dissatisfied, for nothing can fill the vacuum in their life created by those early years of deprivation.

If you are intending to start a relationship with a narcissist, then your only chance of getting along with them, at least in the short term, is to regularly express admiration and love.

Narcissists are almost always over-concerned with their physical appearance. A man with this trait will tend to be highly dissatisfied with his body, and will invariably be discontented with the size of his penis. If he is to enjoy lovemaking, he must have a partner who finds him sexually irresistible. Unless the woman he is with supplies him with plenty of adulation and reassurance, either verbally or via highly pleasurable sexual reactions to his love play, he will feel insecure about his sexual attractiveness or performance. Any lover, however, who is skilled in the art of sexual compliments, will probably be well rewarded for her efforts, as narcissistic men are especially stimulated, both mentally and physically, by any well-chosen sexual praise. Even with such positive reinforcement, however, such individuals rarely remain pleased with themselves for any significant duration, as they generally need new sexual encounters from time to time in order to maintain their sexual morale.

Women with narcissistic signs in their writing are also self-conscious, and are often very critical of their breasts, buttocks or stomach, or of their whole figure, even if they are, by most people's standards, extremely attractive. If she is criticized or undervalued in any way, her sexual ego will be irreparably bruised.

Both male and female narcissists will inevitably look elsewhere for satisfaction if they think their mate is no longer turned on by them, as they are not capable of tolerating this type of blow to their libido.

FAMOUS NARCISSISTS

Marilyn Monroe

Elvis Presley

Michael Jackson

Cassius Clay
(Muhammed Ali)

Elizabeth
Taylor

Sam Houston,
American
General

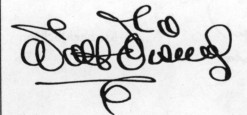

Walt Disney

13. 'Who Me? Never!'

(SIGNS OF TRUTH-STRETCHING)

Signs to look for: Handwriting of **any** style that satisfies one or more of the following points:

1. Legible writing with words missing a whole letter (you need to find three or more words where this happens). This rule does not apply to letters that are missing due to excessive speed of writing.

2. Legible writing with words missing part of a letter so as to alter the identity of that letter. This rule does not apply to the small letters 'e', 'r' or 't' or to parts of letters that are missing due to excessive speed of writing.

3. The small letters 'a', 'c', 'o' or 'g' made with a double or treble loop (check that there are several letters that have this sign).

4. The small letters 'a' or 'o' containing a hook inside.

> *and about or*

5. Writing with many examples of letters that have been written over, in a manner that tends to reduce legibility rather than improving it.

> *and trying to cover up errors*

6. Writing with several examples of lines which have a wavy baseline.

> *sometimes I feel quite unsteady.*

Points 1 and 2 are not valid for the writing of people with dyslexia or other spelling difficulties.

For a description of sexual behaviour patterns and other aspects of personality connected with these indicators, see 'The Devious Loop', page 47.

PART FOUR

Lovers' Portfolio

(PERSONALITY PROFILES OF EVERY TYPE OF LOVER YOU ARE LIKELY TO COME ACROSS)

14. The Potent Lover

Signs to look for: Handwriting of **any style** that satisfies one or more of these points:

1. Writing with at least two examples of the small letter 'g' with a descending line that is three and a half (or more) times the height of the central zone. (This point is not valid if the 'g's are written with a pen pressure that is obviously very light, faded or weak in appearance.)

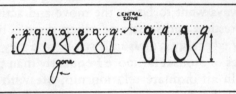

2. Writing with at least two examples of the small letter 'g' with a descending line that is only three times the height of the central zone but, in addition, the writing has one or more of the following four characteristics:

• Writing containing many letters that are clogged with ink.

> *George and Eathy have come*

• Writing which has a muddy, smudgy or smeary appearance.

> *The creading joys of fassionate love.*

- Writing done from choice with a thick felt-tip pen, or any other pen producing broad, thick lines.

feelings Awareness

- Writing where heavy pen pressure makes indentations that clearly show on the reverse of the paper.

Potent lovers possess a naturally high energy level, and an innate determination rooted in a strong survival instinct. They always want to be on the move and active, as they become restless and frustrated when there is little to do. Their sexual energy is unusually strong and they are subject to feelings of arousal far more frequently than the average person. In an intimate relationship, life with them will inevitably be demanding and pressured, unless their partners have similarly high levels of sexual vitality and ambition.

Even in leisure time, they find it almost impossible to sit back, relax and take it easy, for their overactive restless nature is constantly prodding them into action. If they are living with someone who cannot keep up with them, or who is simply a 'laid back' unambitious type with a love of pleasure, they will feel dissatisfied, and be likely to nag and complain, as they consider such behaviour unproductive and intolerably lazy.

Men with the signs of the potent lover in their writing have abundant sexual stamina and no matter how involved they become in their work or other activities they will always place great importance on their sex life, experiencing great frustration and discontentment if deprived of what they consider to be sufficient sex. They will usually desire sexual intercourse on a daily basis, and if their partner has a low sex drive and makes love only very rarely, this will obviously be a source of serious conflict in the relationship. Indeed, in such cases, even if they have a basically loyal nature, their strong appetite for sex will make it very difficult for them to resist if they are presented with an opportunity to satisfy their frustrated sexual desires elsewhere.

A woman of this type will expect her man to be a very capable provider, and if she has a career you can be sure it will be a main priority in her life.

She is bound to also have a good appetite for sex and will certainly appreciate her man being virile, but even if her partner turns out to have a much lower sex drive she will not experience anywhere near the sort of distress that her male equivalent would under the same circumstances. Consequently, in spite of any sexual frustration she might feel, she will be far less prone than her male counterpart to acts of infidelity.

According to Anne Moir and David Jessel (authors of *Brainsex*), and other researchers in the field of human sexuality, there is a strong tendency to promiscuity encoded in the male genes and printed on the brain 'circuitboard' whereas the human female is genetically much less prone to be interested in a variety of partners. (For an explanation of this variance between the sexual behaviour of males and females, see 'Are You In Danger?' page 216.)

Even if she does have promiscuous inclinations, these may well be suppressed as a result of society's double standards for men and women: if a woman is unfaithful or enjoys sex with multiple partners, she is still, even today, liable to be branded as immoral or labelled a nymphomaniac. Consequently sexual frustration in women will often be sublimated instead through work, sport or possibly some creative outlet.

If the writing shows the signs in this chapter, together with even longer stems on the small letter 'g', the behaviour traits are intensified, and the writer will be over-sexed rather than merely potent and the following will apply.

The over-sexed lover is bursting with an almost uncontrollably high energy level, and an unstoppable bulldog-like determination. A powerful survival instinct, a primordial legacy from our Stone Age ancestors, keeps such people permanently on the alert and overactive, and so their 'fight/flight' response is continually being stimulated unnecessarily. Consequently, their bodies are frequently infused with massive amounts of adrenaline to handle emergency situations which in reality rarely exist. This response to the environment would have been wonderfully compatible with life in the Stone Age, but is ill-adapted to the lives of most people today.

In an attempt to release and escape from the enormous build-up of pressure stemming from the overwhelming energy, insecurity and fear connected with this reaction, they have become obsessed with two things in life – sex and their career.

Their ambition knows no limit, and they pursue their objectives with tremendous intensity – when a goal is set they will gladly work around the clock to get things done, using their inexhaustible determination and energy to ignore any signals that indicate that they are placing themselves under excessive stress.

Many individuals with this graphological characteristic find it absolutely essential to allocate on a daily basis sufficient time for at least one hour of hard exercise (indeed, those with such high energy claim that they cannot 'survive' without such a routine).

Anyone with this trait who does not already have a

programme of regular exercise would be well advised to embark on one, as it is of utmost importance for their physical health and psychological sanity that they burn up the massive amounts of adrenaline-based hormones that are overstimulating their whole system.

Finding harmony in a long-term relationship will be almost impossible for these individuals, who tend to be workaholics, and inevitably devote a disproportionate amount of time and attention to their career. This is likely to leave their partners feeling neglected and unimportant, and when they are at home they will be stressful to live with because their restless, hyperactive nature never allows them to relax.

The greatest obstacle hindering them from finding long-lasting happiness in a relationship, however, is their insatiable sexual appetite, which frequently overwhelms even their obsession with work.

A man of this type will require sex every single day, and will consider it as essential to existence as sleeping. At least one repeat performance will be expected during each session, as his sexual desire and vitality is simply overflowing, and once will rarely be sufficient to satisfy him.

It is evident that we are dealing here with someone who will be the ideal match for nymphomaniacs or over-sexed lovers, so anyone with average sexual engineering should stand clear of this individual.

There is at least one major drawback to possessing such an enormous libido however: if this person is sexually deprived, the frustration he experiences will be almost unbearable. If such circumstances do not change he may easily become the victim of severe depression. Such people, therefore, have no chance of finding any sort of contentment in a relationship if they are condemned to living with a partner who has, or suddenly develops, a low sex drive. Many such individuals have strongly polygamous tendencies, and even if they have an intrinsically loyal, faithful nature with a highly developed sense of morals and ethics, their sexual desire is so overwhelmingly intense that it will inevitably succeed in overriding their conscious self-control, and they will find the sight of an aroused and willing female impossible to resist, no matter how guilty it may later make them feel. Infidelity, in this case, is almost forgivable, as the forces of nature have an iron grip on this particular member of the human species.

An over-sexed woman will have as much difficulty as her male counterpart in finding a suitable mate, as not only will she need her man to be exceptionally potent but he will also be expected to be romantic, sensitive and understanding. She will easily become bored with a repetitive lovemaking style.

Her lover will need to blend a careful cocktail of sexual spontaneity and inventiveness, with sensual, romantic sensitivity and abundant virility – a 'tall order' by anyone's standards.

15. The Sex-Crazy Lover

Signs to look for: Handwriting of any style that satisfies one or more of these points:

1. Writing with many examples of the letter 'g' with a stem that has an over-inflated balloon appearance of any shape. The stem must be at least three and a half times the length of the central zone. (This point is not valid if the 'g's are written with a pen pressure that is obviously very light, faded, or weak in appearance.)

2. Writing with many examples of the letter 'g' with a stem that has an over-inflated balloon appearance of any shape, but if the stem is only two and a half times the length of the central zone then, in addition, the writing must show one or more of the following four characteristics:

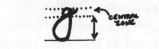

• Writing containing many letters that are clogged with ink.

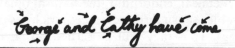

- Writing which has a muddy, smudgy or smeary appearance.

The enduring joys of femininity are here.

- Writing done from choice with a thick felt-tip pen or any other pen producing broad, thick lines.

feelings Awareness

- Writing where heavy pen pressure makes indentations that clearly show on the reverse of the paper.

If you are in search of a soul-mate who loves action, excitement, variety and an abundance of good, healthy sex, then this adventurous spirit may be exactly what you are looking for!

In this individual, extreme intensity of desire combines with a highly active, vivid imagination, and the fusion of these two powerful 'mind forces' creates repercussions which strongly influence virtually every area of the personality and behaviour.

Such people have strong, sensual natures combined with abundant vitality and an insatiable yearning to live life to the full, so self-denial may well be an alien concept to them. They frequently seem to be born with extra sensitive tastebuds, which trigger off unusually high amounts of the 'pleasure chemical' endorphin (the natural opiate released by enjoyable sensual experiences such as eating or lovemaking). Thus they will be turned on far more than most by high-quality cuisine, and are likely to have a real gourmet appetite, indulging themselves whenever possible with fine restaurants or really good home cooking – they will certainly fully appreciate a mate who is a gifted cook.

Unfortunately, though, many people with this characteristic also have a 'live now, pay later' attitude to life that predisposes them to over-indulgence. In such cases, self-destructive habits need to be avoided, as moderation is unlikely to be a part of their vocabulary.

An intimate relationship with someone like this will always be stimulating, but there may be times when the tension runs high and stresses become unbearable. Being ruled by so many desires, such people tend to take on more than they can comfortably handle, and may stress and complicate their lives unnecessarily. This may make them constantly irritable towards their mates, and have devastating effects on the quality of their relationships.

On the positive side, when making progress they can be incredibly enthusiastic, entertaining and generous-hearted and you can be sure they will do their best to make their mates feel on top of the world. Probably the key feature of their personality is their enormous libido, which is incessantly fuelled by a limitless erotic fantasy. There is, however, a significant difference between men and women of this type, in terms of sexual behaviour patterns and fantasy. Men with this characteristic have a sexual imagination that would inspire even the most creative of erotic film producers or authors of sexual literature. Their fantasies in comparison with their female counterparts' will be far more primitive and impersonal; the expression of love and the more sensitive components of foreplay will rarely be a feature of the images which pass through their mind. Often the participants of their inner 'sex show' will be total strangers, maybe someone they have recently seen in a magazine, or passing in the street; alternatively, they may see themselves in action with a vague acquaintance they hardly know, perhaps a woman who travels the same route to work. Fantasies will focus predominantly on the sexual act itself, as they envisage themselves indulging lustful passions in a wide variety of positions and places, sometimes with more than one partner at a time.

Only the most advanced stages of foreplay are likely to be included in their erotic 'shows': visions of themselves administering and receiving steamy oral sex, with close-up views of female genitalia, and scenes where they see themselves in ecstatic intercourse with the woman in the dominant position, are likely to be a popular part of their repertoire.

In an intimate relationship they will obviously be considered extremely demanding unless their lover has an equal sexual appetite. Not only will they desire sex on a daily basis, but they will quickly recover their energy and want at least one repeat performance: they are likely to be the perfect companion for over-sexed lovers. If, however, they are deprived of what they consider sufficient sex, extreme frustration will be experienced, and if things do not change they will become exceedingly depressed.

They have no chance whatsoever of finding any real happiness in life if their partners' sex drive is low, and under such circumstances there is a significant chance that they will look for someone else. Even if they have an essentially faithful nature, their strong appetite for sex and vivid erotic fantasy could well override the conscious self-control mechanisms of the intellect: they will almost certainly succumb to temptation if it crosses their path. If no such opportunity presents itself, or if they are too frightened to look elsewhere, then these types invariably discharge their enormous build-up of sexual tension via compulsive masturbation in the company of their voluptuous fantasy playmates.

Women with this characteristic also have a very powerful sexual appetite, and are just as capable of enjoying the pleasures of sex on a regular basis, but their sexual behaviour patterns are nevertheless somewhat different. If a mate is a poor lover they, too, will feel dissatisfied and somewhat distressed, but will not experience anything like the frustration, depression and irritability that their male counterparts would under the same circumstances. In addition, they are far less prone to infidelity.

A woman with this graphological sign will not only tend to be faithful but, in addition, would be considered by most men to be an extremely satisfying lover. She will, undoubtedly, be sufficiently uninhibited and open-minded to investigate new and exciting approaches to sex, including innovative sexual games and experimental positions derived from oriental sexual practices. Unfortunately, however, she will find it exceptionally difficult to find someone who can satisfy her own needs. She will rapidly tire of any lover who has routine lovemaking patterns, for she needs someone with an essentially romantic, sensitive nature, who is highly sensual as well as sexually spontaneous and inventive. In other words, she will be considerably harder to satisfy sexually than her male counterpart.

Her sexual fantasies will also differ enormously from those of men in the same category. Women's fantasies are far less primitive and considerably more romantic, and invariably take place with someone for whom there are feelings of deep affection. Tender courtship rituals will usually be visualized prior to any sexual imagery, and when the more erotic part of her fantasizing does begin, you can be sure it will include an abundance of touching and sensitive foreplay prior to the act of full penetration.

Women are generally turned on far more by images of power and romance than by physical appearance or animal passion. Fantasies about genuine romantic love will arouse them, not close-ups of the male organ, and impersonal sex devoid of any heartfelt emotion. Their imagined lovers will be figures of achievement in creative, intellectual or monetary terms, and unlike their male counterparts they will rarely envisage themselves having sex with more than one partner. In making love with their real-life partners, such women will sometimes use this capacity for vivid fantasy to turn what might have been only a mediocre orgasm into a stunning one.

Unfortunately, some people of this type seem to experience only negative effects from their vivid erotic imagination. They confuse fantasy with reality, and start believing that they should be able to have sexual experiences in real life that are as perfect and satisfying as the ones they have created in their minds. This comparison, and the unrealistically high expectations it triggers off, causes bitter and sometimes intolerable disappointment.

As a consequence of this unhealthy attitude, immense feelings of sexual frustration arise, which are automatically blamed on the partner, so it is exceptionally difficult for these people to find satisfaction in any monogamous relationship. In such cases, life becomes a ceaseless and futile search for the 'ideal sex mate' as they work their way through numerous dissatisfying experiences.

People with this characteristic have an incredibly friendly social manner, combined with an air of self-assurance which will inspire confidence and trust in those they meet. If, however, you intend beginning a relationship with someone like this, make sure you first probe well beneath the surface, as such people have a natural sense of showmanship as well as a tendency towards exaggeration. Consequently, they could create a very convincing false impression of their qualities and abilities while skilfully hiding facets of personality that may be far less attractive.

If the balloon-shaped stem described in Points 1 or 2 is very noticeably extended to the left (see 'I Wonder... Straight or Gay?' page 205 for clear graphic examples of this variation) you will need to make appropriate and obvious gender changes with regard to the use of personal pronouns and description of male/female body parts, so that the information in this chapter makes sense when read from a homosexual perspective.

16. The Occasional Lover

Sign to look for: Handwriting of any style that satisfies this point:

Clean writing (i.e. not smeary in appearance, or with ink-filled ovals), which is light in pressure (i.e. the pen makes no visible indentations on the reverse of the paper), in which the stem of the letter 'g' is consistently short (less than the height of the central zone). In addition, there must be no examples in the writing of 'g's with a balloon-shaped stem. If the stem of the 'g' is so short that it barely descends below the baseline, everything mentioned in the description below will apply, but the paragraph discussing low sex drive will be accentuated, as this person is also likely to be suffering from problems of impotence. See 'This Has Never Happened To Me Before!' page 190, for further details.

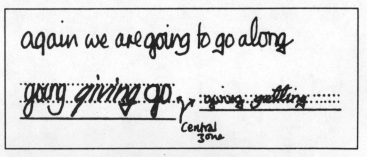

This person has a surprisingly unmaterialistic attitude to existence, so the choice of mate in an intimate relationship is unlikely to be influenced by matters such as financial status. It may be that an economically secure childhood supplied all possible needs, thereby eliminating any strong interest in money, or perhaps the person concerned already has sufficient wealth and feels no need to accumulate more. Alternatively, there may simply be an immature and unrealistic outlook on life and an irresponsible attitude towards planning for the long-term future.

However, if the writing contains the graphological signs shown above but there are also examples of 'y's which have a balloon-shaped stem, this lack of material interests does not apply.

It is very probable that such people have a lower than average level of stamina, and are relatively unconcerned about their physical well-being. As long as they are well enough for their health not to disrupt day-to-day living and working, they will not pay much attention to it.

In an intimate relationship, if their partner has a more than average sex drive, there may well be some tension and conflict arising from sexual incompatibility, for such people's sexual stamina is rather low, and this will inevitably reduce the frequency of their desire to make love. If, however, they are fortunate enough to possess a warm, emotional nature, then they may be able to compensate for their lower than average sexual stamina by satisfying their partner with loving displays of affection.

There are several possible causes for this lower than average libido. In some cases, the cause of the reduced sex drive may be sexual immaturity; indeed this characteristic is seen quite often in the writing of very young teenagers who have not yet developed an adult manner of expressing their sexuality. Alternatively, you may be dealing here with someone who has a poor libido which is the consequence of diminished physical vitality stemming from overwork and/or self-destructive habits such as drinking or smoking. If this is the case, then it is essential that the person makes a decision as soon as possible to change this damaging way of life, or not only health but also the quality of any relationship will be at risk.

Finally, one occasionally comes across people whose reduced interest in sex stems not from emotional immaturity or self-destructive habits but has arisen as a result of some severe life crisis which has destroyed their desire for experiencing any real sexual satisfaction.

If the graphological sign in this chapter appears, but is not a regular feature of the handwriting, this means that the person concerned is going through a purely temporary phase of diminished vitality stemming from a variety of possible sources, such as overwork, stress, lack of sleep, or illness and its after-effects. If this is the case, then this description of personality will only be applicable for the period that the sign shows in their writing.

258

17. The Sublimated Lover

Sign to look for: Handwriting of **any style** which satisfies this point:

The small letter 'g' is consistently written like the small letter 'q' except that the base of the stem must be rounded.

give right dog night

If you are not interested in the sexual side of relationship, but are seeking companionship based on friendship and possibly a mutual interest in matters of philosophy and spirit, then 'hitching up' with this person may well hold the promise of future happiness.

When this graphological sign appears in people's writing, you can be pretty sure that they will communicate with others in a manner ·that exudes sympathy and understanding. Possessing a social conscience and an altruistic streak, such people are highly unlikely ever to turn their backs on a friend in need, and their charitable nature will ensure they are popular in social circles. During the early stages of courtship, their warm responsive manner, and ability to listen with full attention and interest will enable them to establish a friendly rapport remarkably quickly. In a long-term relationship, their good-natured sensitive approach will ensure that they are considerate and responsive, and they will genuinely do their best to attend to their mate's needs.

Although sexual fidelity is today becoming an

increasingly rare commodity, as far as these people go, one need not worry. Firstly, they are likely to possess a strong sense of ethics that would help prevent them from such an act of betrayal, and secondly, their need for sexual contact appears to be rather low, as the energy of their libido is not being expressed in the normal fashion.

These types strongly suppress their sexual impulses, and instead release and redirect this energy through other channels; their sexuality is liable to be sublimated via their career, or perhaps social or altruistic concerns.

It should be clear, therefore, that great conflict will be experienced in their relationships if they are with someone who has a normal, healthy sexual appetite, as it is very unlikely that they will be able to satisfy such needs.

This problem will clearly not exist if their mate is equally uninterested in lovemaking, but if this is not the case, then unresolvable incompatibility is inevitable, and the help of a relationship counsellor should be sought in order to determine if the couple has any real future together.

18. The Kinky Lover

Signs to look for: Handwriting of **any style** which satisfies both these points:

1. Writing with one or more of the following four characteristics:

- Writing containing many letters that are clogged with ink.

> *George and Eathy have come*

- Writing which has a muddy, smudgy, or smeary appearance.

> *The cunding joys of Sexuality in love.*

- Writing done from choice with a thick felt-tip pen, or any other pen producing broad, thick lines.

> *feelings Awareness*

- Writing where heavy pen pressure makes indentations that clearly show on the reverse of the paper, or where there are sudden bursts of heavy pressure.

> *sudden changes are disturbing*

2. Writing which has numerous examples of any of the unusual stem formations of the letter 'g' that are shown below.

If someone's writing has these graphological indicators, there is a good chance the person will enjoy experimenting with a wide variety of unusual sexual practices.

In such a person's daily existence, at work and in social situations it is quite possible that behaviour patterns that are perfectly normal will be displayed, but beneath the exterior is an individual who is often gripped by bizarre sexual fantasies and desires.

Indeed, people in this category will probably indulge in sexual practices which the average person would regard as very strange. Enjoying weird lovers and kinky, erotic sex games, they will be desperately bored by the standard sexual repertoire of the average couple, and will rapidly lose interest in any lover who does not have a vivid sexual imagination, and a love of way-out erotic practices.

Some individuals with kinky inclinations express them only when alone, perhaps via unusual methods of masturbation. Perhaps this is because they believe, or know, that their weird cravings would not be tolerated by a lover.

When spiral formations are seen in lower stems the tendency towards strange sexual tastes is magnified in the extreme. Rarely emotionally honest, these people are easily capable of deceit and infidelity in order to satisfy their lusts. If their mate does not have the same sexual inclinations, they will either leave the relationship for someone else who does or, alternatively, lead a secret, double existence where they can indulge their fantasies freely with others, without their partner's knowledge and interference. Sexually highly eccentric, these people feel that sex is not worth the trouble unless it is bizarre or outrageous, and many of them would be open to the idea of group sex.

Men with this graphological sign are quite likely to enjoy hard-core sex shows, erotic pornographic movies, and explicit pornographic literature, and will find normal sex so unstimulating that in some cases there may even be a difficulty in getting an erection. It is interesting to note that men with weak libidos sometimes purposely cultivate an interest in weird eroticism in order to boost their interest in sex.

Unfortunately, some men with spirals in the lower stems of their writing have a very lowered resistance to sexual excesses or perversions, and will indulge themselves in such practices from time to time. If found out by a partner, this will inevitably cause an unresolvable, permanent rift in the relationship. Indeed, people prone to such acts should seek the immediate help of a sex therapist experienced in the area of abnormal sexual behaviour.

19. The Considerate Lover

Signs to look for: Handwriting of any style that satisfies all the following points:

1. Writing in which the small letter 'g' almost always has a smoothly curved balloon-shaped appearance. The balloon-shaped stem must be proportional looking (not less than the height of the central zone, but not more than one and a half times the height). The information in this chapter does not apply if there are also examples in the same writing of 'g's which have an over-inflated appearance.

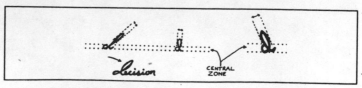

2. Writing with several examples of the small letter 'd' with a looped stem. The looped stem must be proportional looking, not wider than the height of the central zone. The information in this chapter does not apply if there are also examples in the same writing of 'd's which have an over-inflated appearance.

264

3. Writing with many examples of cup-shaped endings on words:

and hid though am at are

4. Writing that leans, even slightly, to the right (writing that leans to the right more than the following example is not valid).

Understanding feelings

5. Writing in which the dot on the small letter 'i' is nearly always small and round.

investigation is limiting his rights!

6. Writing in which the small letters 'a' and 'o' are nearly always very rounded and also clear inside.

good food as always

7. Writing that contains none of the graphological signs listed in Chapters 11 and 12. (To be 100 per cent certain of the accuracy of the personality description given in this chapter, also check Part One, 'The Alphabet of Sex and Relationship', to make sure there are no especially negative signs which offset the contents of this chapter.)

When this combination of graphological characteristics appears in handwriting, there is an excellent chance that the writer will turn out to be sincere and straightforward, candid in opinions and honourable to commitments. In an intimate relationship, such people are invariably very faithful.

They can establish a rapport with people remarkably quickly, thanks to their tremendous empathic abilities which allow them to sense the thoughts and feelings of others with incredible accuracy. They know how to listen sympathetically with full attention and interest, and even on a first meeting they will be able to make a partner feel relaxed and comfortable. This ability to create a relaxed, happy atmosphere should result in a natural progression to the more intimate stages of the courtship ritual.

Sensitive and warm in their approach to lovemaking, they will usually be able to express their feelings of love fairly easily. Possessing an air of self-assurance in their attitude towards sex, they will be able to put at ease even shy and inexperienced lovers, whilst smoothly initiating them into the wide-ranging pleasures of sex.

Such people invariably have a good sexual appetite that is fuelled by a healthy sexual fantasy, and so they are bound to be uninhibited in their manner of lovemaking. Also, their sensitivity to other people's needs has provided them with a very supple sexual nature, so there is every chance they will be exceptionally entertaining partners in bed. Indeed, their skill in adapting their style of lovemaking should enable them to satisfy a wide range of sexual appetites. During foreplay, their sensitive nature will allow them to tune into and respond to each erotic zone in turn, whilst noticing and responding to all the subtle nuances of their mate's reactions, until he or she reaches a peak of pleasurable arousal.

In intimate relationships with people who are reasonably compatible with them, sexually and emotionally, they will display a warm, romantic, loving nature, and under such circumstances there is a very high chance that they will be able to remain faithful through life to one partner.

During leisure time these individuals will undoubtedly want to enjoy an active social life, entertaining guests at home, or going to parties. If their partners happen to be the type who love privacy and dislike socializing, there will obviously be very significant conflict of interests. Indeed, to deprive these characters of an ample social life is to destroy any chances they might have of a happy existence.

20. The Humorous Lover

Signs to look for: Handwriting of **any style** that satisfies one or more of these points:

1. Writing containing several examples of a wavy line or a 'smile' line. These may appear in any of the following places in someone's writing:

a. In the underlining of a person's signature:

b. On capital or small letters:

c. In the connections between letters:

2. Writing in which the small letter 'g' is often shaped like a number 8.

3. Writing containing several examples of letters with upper stems that form a 'bent over' loop that is lying close to the central zone.

CENTRAL ZONE

4. Many wide loops in the upper stems of letters, in writing where the lines generally ascend the page.

Do you believe it is absolutely essential for a lover to have a good sense of humour? If so, then this graphological characteristic should be a welcome sign, as it always discloses someone who has a great potential to see the funny side of life.

The ability to see the ridiculous side of things will prove to be a valuable tool for patching up any areas of conflict in an intimate relationship. When emotions reach boiling point, people like this sometimes have the knack of being able to crack the right sort of joke, or do something silly to transmute the tense atmosphere into one of laughter.

When their partners are feeling down, they will invariably come up with some amusing observation or comment or simply act the fool in order to elevate their spirits.

As long as there are no major sexual problems or inhibitions in the relationship, then this sense of comedy should significantly enhance lovemaking. Indeed, there is even a physiological basis for this: humour releases endorphins, the body's natural opiates. These chemicals of relaxation, sensuality and pleasure considerably enhance the feeling of well-being and enjoyment in all areas of life, including sex.

Also, according to the teachings of oriental sexual yoga, the lower stomach, or *'Svadhisthana Chakra'*, as it is called, is the centre of sexual energy. Stimulating this *Chakra* in various ways, with breathing and other exercises, considerably increases one's sexual desire. Genuine laughter causes this whole area to pump in and out vigorously, thereby activating not only the endorphins but also the sexual energy stored in this centre. In other words, laughing can be a real turn on (which clearly explains the aphrodisiac qualities that many people ascribe to humour).

People with a light-hearted manner towards sex will have no trouble in melting any initial shyness at the start of a new relationship. If they also have a vivid erotic fantasy, they may well derive great amusement from experimenting with the numerous and often hilariously funny lovemaking positions of the *Kama Sutra*.

Indeed, sex for some of these types is simply an endless source of laughs, and such individuals need to be careful not to carry things too far, or they may end by upsetting a partner's passionate, romantic advances with an inappropriate joke or an outburst of misplaced laughter.

If the writing shows the signs in this chapter but in addition it contains graphological indicators from any of the following three chapters: 'I Could Never Do This With My Partner!', 'The Occasional Lover' and 'The Sublimated Lover', the description of humour will only apply to the non-sexual side of the relationship, and all the information pertaining to sexual behaviour should be disregarded.

21. The Sensual Lover

Signs to look for: Handwriting of **any style** that satisfies **both** these points:

1. Writing with one or more of the following four characteristics:

• Writing containing many letters that are clogged with ink.

> *George and Cathy have come*

• Writing which has a muddy, smudgy or smeary appearance.

> *The unending joys of sensuality are here.*

• Writing done from choice with a thick felt-tip pen, or any other pen producing broad, thick lines.

> **feelings Awareness**

• Writing where heavy pen pressure makes indentations that clearly show on the reverse of the paper.

2. Writing that does not have any of the graphological indicators from the following three chapters: 'I Could

Never Do This With My Partner!', 'The Occasional Lover' and 'The Sublimated Lover'.

Controlling the physical appetites could pose a problem for this individual, who is very strongly ruled by the primal, instinctive desire that our species has for sensual pleasures.

Possessing extra-sensitive tastebuds, such people will certainly love their food and drink, and their highly sensual nature has provided them with a real passion for sex.

In the midst of pleasure, these types are prone to feeling shivering sensations traversing the length of their spines. This physical response is the sign of an 'endorphin rush'. Endorphins are internally produced chemicals which are responsible for the feelings of elation that accompany enjoyable activities, both physical and sensual. People with the graphological signs of 'The Sensual Lover' seem to produce unusually high amounts of these 'pleasure chemicals', and this perhaps explains their strong appetites for food and sex, as well as the tremendous natural 'high' they experience in the aftermath of such pleasures. You can be quite sure that they will seek out every possible opportunity to stimulate their senses to the maximum in both of these areas, and it will come as no great surprise if they sometimes exhibit behaviour that could only be described as decadently over-indulgent.

If you intend dating such a person and are wondering how best to spend the time, then you could not do better than suggest a night out at a choice restaurant that serves mouth-wateringly delicious food, amid an atmosphere of fine music and soft, sensuous lighting. This will break the ice and set things on track almost right from the start, and if everything goes as well as expected it could easily lead to a mutual unspoken understanding that the evening is destined for sexual intimacy. If this is indeed the case, then the perfect hors d'oeuvre on arriving home, sure to whet the appetite of this sensual gourmet, would be a warm, scented bath for two, filled with bubbles, and light-hearted, sensuous fun. Follow this with sexy music in combination with a mutual intimate massage with warm oil, and the scene will be set for one of the greatest-ever bedtime stories.

Remarkably responsive to tactile stimulation, the sexual feelings of this sensual lover will be easily aroused, and whilst touching, caressing and exploring every inch of your body, this pheromone connoisseur will seem almost inebriated by the unique sexual aromas of your excited, erotic passions.

It should be quite clear from this personality portrait that people with the above-mentioned characteristics will often turn out to be passionate, sensual, imaginative and exciting in their style of lovemaking and so, if their partners do not share their love of sex and pleasurable living, this could result in a grave incompatibility. They also need to guard against a tendency to excesses, which could lead to self-destructive patterns of living.

In addition, it should be noted that some people in this category are so powerfully addicted to sex that they may find it extremely difficult to remain faithful in a monogamous relationship. If their partner is away from home for a few days or more, and someone they find attractive makes them a tempting offer, it will be almost impossible for them simply to say no.

Finally, if you are considering a relationship with one of these people, you should be aware that when angry they can demonstrate a fiery, explosive temper, and if the writing is dark and smeary (note the relevant sample above) this may indicate a tendency towards violence in the personality, and in very extreme cases could also show a predisposition towards sexual perversion.

22. The Emotionally Switched-off Lover

Sign to look for: Handwriting of any style that satisfies this point:

Writing that leans to the left as much or more than this:

to keep my emotions private

feelings are difficult to express

rarely live up fully to ones original expectations

This person's feelings are strongly suppressed and carefully hidden, owing to mistrustfulness of others and a preference for avoiding the vulnerability that goes hand in hand with being emotionally open. This approach to life forces such people into a state of inner isolation and, even when surrounded by family and friends, they often experience a deep-rooted sense of loneliness. Many such individuals, however, hide this fact behind a well-polished facade that may create the false impression that they are content, friendly and communicative.

In relationship, their choice of a long-term partner will rarely be determined by a head-over-heels-in-love emotional reaction, as they will cautiously consider the appropriateness of their choice, having first carefully assessed matters such as financial and family background, current social status, physical appearance, etc.

These people harbour strong fears of deep emotional involvement and will rarely, if ever, open their hearts up to a mate. Indeed, they can be so busy suppressing and controlling their own behaviour that they are often completely out of touch with other people's feelings, and are likely to seem very cold and insensitive at times, and lacking in sympathy and compassion.

They fear being rejected, and are frequently filled with doubts about the genuineness of any affection they receive from others. They themselves will rarely, if ever, display any spontaneous feelings of heartfelt love as, even if inwardly they are experiencing such emotions, these will be suppressed by their over-controlled nature. Living with an individual like this can be extremely unnerving at times, as it becomes increasingly difficult to respond in a positive manner to such an emotionally reserved and often undemonstrative human being.

Men with the graphological characteristic have a tendency to treat lovemaking simply as a physical need to be satisfied, as well as an opportunity to test and confirm their virility, in order to boost their ego or allay any insecurities they may have concerning their male prowess. Foreplay will tend to be stilted and predictable, and they are unlikely to be genuinely concerned with providing their partner with sensual and sexual satisfaction, unless it is for the purposes of enhancing their own sexual self-esteem. It probably comes as no great surprise to learn at this stage that men in this category often prefer to devote most of their time and attention to their careers rather than to their intimate relationships, as they are unable to derive sufficient fulfilment from this area of their life.

Women with backward-leaning writing are often attracted to much older men, perhaps due to an unconscious desire for the sort of security and protection that is frequently associated with a father-figure. They usually have a very matter-of-fact attitude towards sex, which they view in a rather detached manner. For many such women, lovemaking is just another one of those many components of an intimate relationship that one needs to deal with. They will expect their partner to make all the moves, as they are usually content to play a somewhat passive role. Indeed, even the most affectionate of lovers will have great difficulty in eliciting a romantic response from them. Even if they enjoy lovemaking, they will nevertheless be in full control of themselves and will, generally speaking, not suffer any great frustration if their sex life is fairly sparse (unless they also show the graphological signs which reveal a very high sex drive).

23. The Emotionally Volatile Lover

Sign to look for: Handwriting **of any style** that satisfies this point:

Writing with most of its letters joined together, leaning so far to the right that it appears to be falling over. (See 'The Jealous Lover', page 296 for further information on this writing feature.)

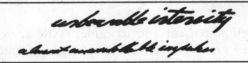

This person experiences life with incredible intensity. Emotions run very deep, and there is total involvement in events. Consequently, such people easily become excited, and are often inclined to highly impulsive behaviour, and extreme reactions to people and circumstances. This emotional structure has made them subject to sudden, powerful mood swings. They can be in a great state of mind one minute, and then without any warning their feelings can abruptly change and they may become very depressed or perhaps fiercely angry. On meeting this person for the first time, you could easily be forgiven if you failed to notice this extremely volatile temperament, for in many such individuals attempts at self-restraint have precipitated an oscillation between extreme over-control on some occasions (which may possibly create the illusion of emotional balance) and complete loss of emotional equilibrium, displaying extremely impulsive behaviour as well as almost hysterical outbursts of anger and frustration, at other times.

These types need plenty of love and attention from their mates, for they are emotionally highly dependent, and without such displays of warmth and affection they tend to feel extremely uneasy and insecure.

Quite clearly, a pressured life style should be avoided at all costs, for their deep emotional relationship with life has submerged any capacity for detachment they might have. This has given them an especially low tolerance for stress, and consequently whenever they are under any sort of pressure this usually precipitates a complete loss of psychological balance, leading to neurotic emotional eruptions.

With their impatient and irritable, restless, excitable nature, they are very vulnerable to negative emotional atmospheres, and simply cannot tolerate any form of hostility. Anyone who dares to cross them will certainly live to regret it. When in a good mood, however, they can be genuinely sentimental and romantic, expressing abundant love and devotion, and an overpowering enthusiasm for sex. Under such conditions, they are capable of radiating tremendous heartfelt warmth and powerful sexual passions, and so their style of foreplay and lovemaking is likely to be intense and exciting. Their level of sexual arousal can at times rise to stupendous proportions and (assuming they have a healthy sex drive and a sexually compatible lover) their experience of orgasm is likely to reach an earth-shattering intensity.

If, however, they are offended by a partner or the emotional climate takes a change for the worse, they will lose all objectivity and reason, and be overwhelmed by a veritable tornado of negative emotional energy. This will inevitably destroy any sense of objectivity or perspective they may have and in such instances, unless the partner remains passive, vicious shouting matches could well ensue.

At such times there will obviously be little or no chance of any form of sexual intimacy occurring, as the atmosphere will be filled with fiercely expressed anger, and even hatred. Indeed, if there are other signs in the writing of poor emotional self-control, revealed perhaps by muddy writing or writing with a confused, restless appearance, then this anger may even take the form of physically violent outbursts.

People of this type generally burn up such enormous reserves of energy with their over-aroused nature that they are bound to frequently feel emotionally burnt out and physically exhausted, and consequently many of them are very prone to over-indulge in various stimulants such as coffee, cigarettes or alcohol.

If you are considering a relationship with this person, think twice, unless very serious steps are already being taken to deal with his or her over-emotional nature, with the help of psychotherapy, meditation or perhaps some other beneficial self-awareness technique.

24. The Moody Lover

Sign to look for: Handwriting of any style that satisfies this point:

Writing in which lines, words or letters or any combination of these lean in different directions, or writing that has a generally restless, messy appearance, caused by factors such as disturbed rhythm, poorly formed letters, uneven baselines or changing letter sizes or style etc.

• Lines leaning in different directions.

> *my emotions seem to control me completely*
> *at other times I just feel detached from it all.*

• Words leaning in different directions.

> *attitudes change moment to moment*

• Letters leaning in different directions.

> *feel so inwardly restless*

• Any other type of writing that has an extremely restless, messy appearance.

This person will be difficult to live with, being temperamental and restless much of the time and with unpredictable moods, so that a partner will never know what to expect. Love life with such individuals will be a real roller-coaster ride. Their sexual nature at one moment can be warm and passionate and then suddenly, without any warning and often for no explicable reason, they will become cold and uninterested. This will obviously be extremely unnerving for anyone they are living with.

Sometimes, in those rare moments when the relationship is running smoothly and there is a flow of mutual good feeling, lovemaking may well turn out to be great (assuming the sex drive of both parties is reasonably normal). Under such conditions, these people are capable of expressing genuine heartfelt warmth and strong sexual passions, and their style of foreplay and lovemaking is likely to be full of the freshness of spontaneously expressed loving feelings.

At other times, however, when their mood takes a sharp and sudden swing for the worse and communication channels are disrupted by angry emotions, there will be little or no chance of any form of sexual intimacy occurring.

This changeable temperament is likely to be a product of a childhood made unhappy by dissension between parents with extremely different and incompatible personalities. The people concerned probably felt unloved and neglected as a result of these family tensions, and in addition may have felt guilty and responsible in some way. Their emotions towards their parents and those around them were often torn between feelings of love and feelings of strong resentment. This emotional disharmony, never resolved, still remains alive and active in their subconscious, and it is this undercurrent of negative emotional energy that is the source of their rapid and often inexplicable mood swings and their capacity to become highly emotional without any provocation.

(See 'The Emotionally Volatile Lover', page 277 for further characteristics connected with moodiness.)

25. The Confused Lover

Sign to look for: Handwriting of **any style** that satisfies this point:

The small letter 'g' with the descending line overlapping with the line below (look for many 'g's that do this).

This writing characteristic discloses a very physically minded, sensual individual with loads of energy, ambition and determination. Often creative, these types love constant variety and change and, if they have the money and opportunity, will travel as often as possible. Possessing inspiration and drive enough for several people, their lively, energized personality just adores action and excitement. In social settings they could well be inclined towards extroverted behaviour, expressing themselves in a colourful, dramatic manner, while stretching the truth to enhance their description of events.

Such individuals have a powerful yearning to express themselves in both speech and action and frequently will turn out to be highly gregarious, capable of enjoying the company of a wide variety of people from all walks of life.

Unfortunately, however, it often happens that people with this graphological characteristic end up fulfilling very little of their potential in life, as they may well suffer from highly confused thinking, and if so, will end up unnecessarily complicating their existence. Frequently such types are overwhelmed by a barrage of conflicting impulses, instincts and desires which create in them psychological instability and tremendous inner disharmony. The more 'tangled' the stems are in the handwriting, the greater the degree and manifestation of their emotional, psychic and mental confusion. A thousand and one ideas arouse their interest and imagination, and they yearn to explore them all. Their hearts are torn between so many unexpressed conflicting feelings that at times the intensity of these frustrated emotions becomes almost unbearable.

Intimate relationships with such people will probably be a heavy ordeal. Sometimes quite infantile in their manner, they seem to find it impossible to get their priorities right; indeed that old cliché 'can't see the wood for the trees' is definitely appropriate here. Their minds are overloaded with too many simultaneous thoughts and plans, which cloud their judgment and destroy their ability to view things objectively. Their evaluation of the reality facing them thus becomes highly subjective and inevitably inaccurate, and so they are very prone to making unwise decisions.

Such people need to find a mate who can harness, control and direct them so that they do not waste their time and energy in the pursuit of pointless enterprises. Emotionally they can be very demanding, as they feel extremely insecure about their ability to cope with life's demands, and may become overdependent on a mate, creating a somewhat claustrophobic atmosphere in the relationship. In addition, the intensity of their personality is likely to make them tiring to be with, although this will be compensated for to some extent by their ability to be very lively and entertaining when they are in a good mood.

This neurotic condition of the psyche was almost

certainly precipitated during childhood by unfulfilled emotional needs, which left the person feeling inadequate and unimportant. In their attempts to escape from this inner suffering and regain a sense of power and self-worth, many such individuals develop an exaggerated desire for money, possessions and prestige. They are inclined to be very preoccupied with sex, and are unlikely to have any inhibitions in this area. They possess a strong sexual appetite, so if a partner does not have a good sex drive this will disappoint and frustrate them a great deal.

Generally speaking, men with this graphological sign find it very difficult to remain faithful to their partners for an extended period, and so any woman who intends starting a relationship with someone like this needs first to discuss this matter with him to find out where she stands.

26. The Workaholic Lover

Signs to look for: Handwriting of any style that satisfies one or more of these points:

1. The small letter 'g' with the descending line appearing to be pulled to the right (look for many examples of 'g's that do this).

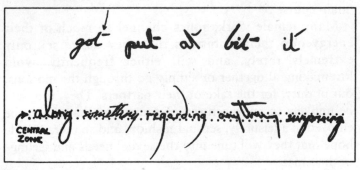

2. The small letter 't' with the crossbar on the right detached from the stem in writing where the central zone is as small or smaller than this (you will need to see several 't's like this).

3. Illegibility of letters in many words caused by writing too fast.

This person will be very difficult to live with because this graphological characteristic usually discloses someone who is a classic example of a workaholic. Relationships with such people will almost definitely be very stressful as their restless, over-active nature rarely, if ever, allows them to relax and being constantly stressed may well cause them to be impatient and irritable on a frequent basis. They will have little time available for a partner, and their concern for the future and their career will inevitably rob them of the opportunity to really enjoy the pleasures of the moment.

It will probably come as no great surprise to learn that their style of lovemaking is unlikely to be particularly impressive. Men with this trait will tend to treat sex as a mere stress release, rather than a sensual pleasure, and their style of foreplay is likely to be almost the same on each occasion, lacking in spontaneity and handled more like a process they are obliged to go through in order to get to the 'main course'.

Many female workaholics channel so much of their energy into their ambitions that they desire sex only extremely rarely, and will either frequently avoid lovemaking altogether or simply go through the motions, out of duty, for the sake of their partners. They, too, will be unlikely to approach sex as something that should be enjoyed in a leisurely, sensual fashion, and so there is little hope that they will tune into the sexual needs and feelings of their mates.

Although people with graphological indications of the workaholic generally have a very adult and reliable attitude towards work and social obligations, their understanding of emotional and sexual matters, as well as other responsibilities involved in relationships, is generally somewhat undeveloped and immature. On the surface they may seem to communicate quite adequately with members of the opposite sex. In fact, however, they lack maturity, sensitivity and understanding in this area. They just do not seem to realize or accept that taking care of their mates' needs and feelings is as important, or even more important, than personal ambition. This egocentric comprehension of existence is difficult to live with, and is liable to make a partner feel rather unimportant, neglected and unloved.

No matter how successful these people become with regard to career and other ambitions, they will never have any chance of achieving a satisfying, harmonious relationship, unless their attitude to life changes completely. They need to develop their awareness and understanding to the point where they realize that relationships must come first in their list of priorities. The root of such people's difficulties lies in a childhood that fostered in them a sense of low self-esteem. The desire to succeed has become such an overwhelming influence in their lives that ambitious thoughts now dominate their consciousness to the exclusion of almost everything else. They are possessed by deep-rooted fears and anxieties that are the symptoms of an over-demanding ego which is constantly telling them that their current position in life is grossly inadequate. Consequently, there is a massive gap between where they are and where they would like to be and, because of this exaggerated distance between their egos and 'ego-ideals', they are destined to be eternally frustrated by their futile attempts to achieve the impossible. Their restless, over-motivated nature is impatient for success, and they are willing to pay a high price for it, working around the clock if necessary, to get things done.

Any warning signals indicating that workaholics are pushing themselves too far and damaging their physical and psychological health are simply ignored as their inner wisdom is usually submerged in a sea of stress and tension that has become familiar territory for them.

Workaholics typically have excessive amounts of adrenaline coursing through their bloodstream, and if this is not burnt up physically the resulting stress could, in the long term, easily damage their health.

27. The Domineering Lover

Signs to look for: Handwriting of **any** style that satisfies one or more of these points:

1. Writing with several examples of the small letter 't' with a crossbar sloping noticeably downwards.

but date but hit cat sit

2. Writing with heavy pen pressure (e.g. the indentations show clearly on the reverse of the paper) in which the small letters 'h', 'm' and 'n' are nearly always sharply angled at the top and bottom.

mahogany WOMAN

This person has a very domineering nature, and in an intimate relationship will always strive hard to achieve a position of control.

Being rigid and inflexible in their attitudes, once such people make up their mind about something, it will be virtually impossible to get them to change it. Their behaviour is highly pedantic and in discussions, if a partner tries to disagree with them in any way they are liable to become very argumentative. Much conflict and argument is inevitable if the partner has the strength of personality to oppose this attempt at domination.

When instructions or orders are issued, if their wishes are not complied with they are likely to become highly irritable, and will attempt to dominate a partner by attacking his or her self-esteem.

These people are likely to have been harshly judged and criticized in childhood by an unsympathetic parent. This treatment will have led to feelings of inadequacy which in adult life cause this desire for control.

Men with the graphological signs in this chapter find it very difficult to take no for an answer when they are in the mood for sex and, if their sexual cravings are very strong, they may well be inclined to make use of their superior physical strength in order to encourage their lover to succumb to their wishes.

A woman with this writing sign is likely to be very critical of her partner and may often deny him sex if she is not satisfied with his performance. If, however, she is pleased by her lover, she will be forward and uninhibited in letting him know exactly what she wants him to do.

28. The Tyrannical Lover

Sign to look for: Handwriting of any style that satisfies this point:

Writing with several examples of the small letter 'g' with a stem that forms a sharply angled triangle of any shape.

If you are a strong supporter of democracy and believe that this value should extend to the home environment, then avoid this particular personality like the plague! For you are dealing here with someone who is without a doubt a domestic tyrant (though this fact might only be evident to those who know the person extremely well).

Relationships with people of this type will often be emotionally very demanding and stressful, as they will be authoritarian, self-righteous and demanding, and will become very annoyed if their position of power is questioned or their expectations not satisfied. In such instances, they can be very fault-finding and in order to strengthen their dominance they may well use subtle manipulations to make others feel guilty, and will attack the vulnerable spots of the ego to undermine self-esteem. Partners will be expected to conform closely to these tyrants' own standards of behaviour, and they will have an exceptionally low tolerance of conduct they consider incorrect. Their rigid, obstinate nature makes it very difficult for them to accept that they might sometimes be wrong, so don't expect them to compromise when they have a difference of opinion with their partners. When these individuals make up their minds about something, or embark upon a particular course of action, they rigidly and dogmatically adhere to it, and a bad atmosphere or argument is a certainty if their partners make any attempt to alter this way of thinking or acting.

People like this will vehemently argue to defend their views and decisions, and will rarely be the one to give in and apologize first. They just love it when they get their own way, and become easily frustrated and irritable if their control over others is undermined or threatened. If this frequently happens they may become permanently sulky or grumpy.

On the positive side, there is every chance that they will be the type who will stand by the side of a loved one when faced with danger or hardship, and in general these people can be relied upon to cope very successfully in situations that demand a sharp survival instinct. There is every chance that they will be a good provider of material security as they possess a strong urge to win, combined with plenty of determination and natural fighting spirit.

An incredibly tense atmosphere is inevitable, however, if such a person's partner has an extremely powerful personality and assumes the dominant position in the relationship. A union like this is liable to have an extremely limited life expectancy. To avoid tremendous friction in a relationship, this person needs a mate who has an unrebellious nature and a great respect for authority.

A perfect example of this would be a woman with a 'slave-type' mentality who is prepared to worship a male tyrant and fall obediently into line, blindly following orders. Ideally, she should also passively accept disrespectful and unfair treatment and do as she is told, irrespective of whether she thinks the instruction right or wrong. Dignity, self-respect and standing up for her beliefs will clearly be undesirable characteristics, which this dictatorial regime would rapidly and ruthlessly strive to crush.

It is extremely likely that this rather undesirable pattern of behaviour has roots in a childhood that was governed by a strong-willed, domineering mother-figure with a sharply critical, judgmental tongue. These early years shaped a psyche filled with repressed anger and resentment as well as feelings of inadequacy and low self-worth. The desire for dominance is simply a futile attempt to escape such emotions.

With regard to their sex lives, such people feel a strong sense of unfulfilment and disappointment. A woman with this graphological sign in her writing is likely to be a classic example of the 'nagging wife' type, and in addition there is a high likelihood that she will have a streak of prudishness towards sex, with rigid ideas concerning bedroom etiquette. A partner who oversteps the boundaries or refuses to conform to her standards will without doubt be denied sexual satisfaction. If a mate disappoints her in the area of morals or ethics, or if she lacks respect for him, then she will very rarely make love and instead will sublimate her sexual energies in some other way, perhaps through her work.

Usually, a man with this graphological sign has highly ambivalent feelings towards the opposite sex. One side of his nature admires women and is attracted to them sexually and emotionally; he might even be exceptionally charming and friendly in their company. Underneath this, however, he is repressing from his conscious awareness an undercurrent of unhealthy emotions towards the female species in general, whom he regards with mistrust and anger. He has a subconscious desire to punish women, to use them as scapegoats for the pent-up bitterness and resentment he felt towards his mother-figure.

If such a person has a high sex drive, then extreme frustration will be experienced if he is deprived of what he considers to be his 'rights'. Under such circumstances he can become very irritable, and will attempt to make his partner feel guilty, or manipulate her in some other way in order to drive her into submission, so that he can get what he wants. He may even, on occasion, resort to violence.

Only in very rare cases will men with this graphological sign turn out to be good lovers. Usually they are so concerned with demonstrating how manly and virile they are in their lovemaking that they fail to accurately tune in to the needs and desires of their mate.

Finally, if you are contemplating a relationship with such a person, or are already in the early stages of an enjoyable relationship with one, take note of the following. These individuals may appear to be perfectly charming during the early stages of courtship, but once they feel sure that someone is emotionally very attached or dependent on them, the control-oriented aspects of their nature will start to emerge. Very rapidly, they will ease themselves into a position of total dominance in the relationship, and the other person's wishes and desires will immediately become secondary to their own.

If the triangular stem on the letter 'g' is noticeably extended to the left (note the last 'g' in the given examples), the following also applies in addition to all the above.

When these people are wronged in some way, they will not just 'forgive and forget' as they have a marked tendency to bear grudges. In relationships, if a nasty remark is addressed to them that was not really meant but simply said in the heat of an argument, they will sulk for an extended period, and their hearts will be filled with bitter feelings of resentment and self-pity. The feeling of resentment towards the mother-figure mentioned earlier is, in this case, considerably accentuated. Seeds of unresolved hostility, planted during the childhood years, without doubt form the roots of this person's current grudge-bearing nature, and it will be very difficult to overcome this negative conditioning without the assistance of psycho-therapy. In a long-term relationship this characteristic will be a source of much pain and suffering, and under such circumstances the chances of a healthy and happy sex life are extremely remote.

29. The Jealous Lover

Signs to look for: Handwriting of **any** style that satisfies one or more of the following points:

1. Writing in which most of the letters within words are joined together, leaning so far to the right that it appears to be falling over.

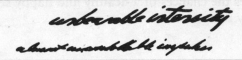

2. Writing with several examples of capitals or small letters with a small circular attachment to the beginning of the letter.

Malta Eva Gone fat sea wit

3. Writing with several examples of capitals or small letters with any squared loop attachment (large or small) to the beginning of the letter.

May Jane Gone few Sea Week

4. Writing that has a very jagged, zig-zag appearance, written with such heavy pen pressure that the indentations can be clearly seen on the reverse of the paper.

I am coming home now

5. Writing done from choice with a thick felt-tip pen (or any other pen producing broad, thick lines) in which the letters within words are widely spaced.

powerful emotions

6. Writing with a restless, messy look caused by an alternating slant, in combination with capital letters in the writing which are very large and showy, and written with such heavy pen pressure that the indentations can be clearly seen on the reverse of the paper.

7. Writing which has at least two of the following points (the more points found, the more extreme the jealousy).

• Writing with numerous examples of letters containing a hook on the right side. Hooks may be large or small.

C R J a c d e f h s t y

• Writing with many examples of looped 'g' stems where the end of the ascending line turns downwards below the baseline.

g g g g g g g g

• Writing with several examples of the letters 'a' and/or 'o' that are considerably larger than other formations in the central zone.

dog year doing eat cane

- Writing with many examples of endings on words which curl back leftwards over the letter.

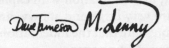

- A signature with an ending stroke that curls back over the top of at least four of the letters in the signature.

Jealousy and possessiveness are the hallmarks of this personality. In social situations this person will be on red alert, and quick to notice any behaviour which might signal potential infidelity. Even the innocent enjoyment of another's conversation may ignite the underlying fear and emotional insecurity that forms the basis of this jealous nature.

The sexual behaviour patterns of such individuals will vary dramatically, depending upon how secure they are feeling with a lover. Some people with this characteristic make dramatic efforts to improve the quality of their sex life if they feel their relationship is under threat. Others in the same situation react in an entirely opposite manner, and 'cold shoulder' their partner or confront them with an outburst of jealous rage: all forms of intimacy are denied until the problem is resolved.

A man with this graphological characteristic might well question his partner in detail about her past affairs and relationships, and there is likely to be a morbid curiosity about the sexual prowess of these former lovers. He inevitably will be concerned that his own virility and sexual performance might not compare favourably. Plenty of reassurance will be needed from his partner to relieve his fears in this area.

It has been suggested by various psychologists that individuals who are very prone to jealous feelings are suffering from an inferiority complex formed during childhood. This may have been precipitated by competition between siblings for parental affection or, if the individual was an only child, then perhaps there was rivalry with one parent for the other parent's love and attention.

In my own personal opinion, however, the roots of jealousy may well stretch back to the time of our earliest ancestors. Perhaps this powerful emotion formed part of the survival pattern of Stone Age man, stimulating whenever required a fierce protectiveness that helped safeguard loved ones from abduction by other tribal members or potential aggressors from different communities. The emotion of jealousy is, however, no longer a useful asset, and seems to be incompatible with the more evolved consciousness and social life style of modern civilization. Indeed, behaviour associated with jealousy is now considered to be an attack on the personal rights and freedom of others.

Someone living with a jealous lover clearly needs to be on his or her guard, especially if this characteristic is seen in combination with any graphological signs suggesting even the possibility of physical aggression. (See 'Are You In Danger?', page 216.)

PART FIVE

What's the Score in Bed?

30. Assessing Sexual Compatibility

Woody Allen has described sex as 'the most fun you can have without laughing'. But sex is not merely fun: sexual harmony is of crucial importance in building an enduring and satisfying intimate relationship. Indeed, the first moment of attraction between two healthy persons of the opposite sex is often based almost exclusively on sexual desire.

Although in the 1960s there was an explosion in sexual promiscuity, the advent of Aids has now curbed much of this sexually liberated enthusiasm, which has been replaced by fear. As a result, many people are beginning to take a fresh look at the advantages of monogamy. Clearly, it is now extremely important to know how to identify a sexually compatible mate as rapidly as possible, in order to avoid the health risks that are inevitable if one is obliged to experiment with numerous partners to find an ideal lover. This chapter provides an effective and easy-to-use method of determining whether or not a couple is sexually compatible.

The quality of a couple's lovemaking and hence their compatibility is determined by the degree of similarity or difference between them in four areas: 1. Raw sexual energy/desire. 2. Sensuality. 3. Sexual imagination/openness. 4. Emotional make-up. The key area however is undoubtedly the first. If a couple has good compatibility in this main area then any incompatibilities that may exist in any of the other three areas should be fairly easy to resolve. If, however, there is a significant incompatibility between a couple in this key area then there may be serious problems in the relationship if there is also disharmony in any of the other areas.

During the early stages of a relationship, it is usually impossible for people to assess their sexual compatibility, as the excitement of newly found love tends invariably to camouflage any potential differences. Indeed, it is not uncommon for someone who normally may have only a very low sex drive to experience temporarily a voracious sexual appetite at the start of a fresh romance. Consequently it is often only much later that a couple may suddenly discover a large discrepancy between their sexual preferences, which can lead to considerable tensions and conflict.

In addition, many couples involved in long-term relationships who are experiencing sexual disharmony refuse to acknowledge this to one another, either because they are too inhibited to do so or because they consciously deny the fact. Instead they blame other areas of their relationship that are usually in no way connected.

If an analysis of your own and your partner's writing alerts you to a significant difference in sexual appetites, this at least gives you a chance to deal with the situation in an open and direct manner. Problems approached with tolerance and a sense of humour can often be solved, and may even serve to strengthen a relationship. The reader should also be aware of 'desire discrepancy', a common phenomenon. Research into human sexual behaviour patterns has shown that in the majority of heterosexual relationships the man has a significantly higher sex drive than the woman. This difference in desire seems to be part of our human condition, and endocrinologists believe it is a consequence of the much higher level in males of the hormone testosterone, which has been directly linked with the sex drive in both humans and other animal species. This fact obviously needs to be taken into account when measuring the sex drive of two individuals. If you discover, when assessing the level of a couple's sexual energy/desire, that they have identical scores, although they can be classed as sexually highly compatible in this area, the influence of the 'desire discrepancy' factor will mean that the man is likely to want sex a little more often than his partner. If, however, the female in the relationship scores a little higher in terms of sexual energy, this would tend to compensate for the usual biological difference between the sexes, and one could expect to find an almost perfect match with regard to the frequency of desire for lovemaking.

Finally, any method or system of knowledge that claims it can determine compatibility in relationship would be misrepresenting itself if it failed to acknowledge its significant failing in one mysterious yet seemingly highly important area. Recent scientific research into the biological basis of behaviour lends further weight to those age-old comments regarding sexual attraction which talk about the 'chemistry' between a couple being right or wrong. Human beings are constantly sending off chemical signals known as pheromones. These are extremely subtle odours that we cannot consciously smell but which nevertheless are detected by odour receptors responding at a subconscious level of our awareness. Every individual secretes his or her own particular cocktail of pheromone chemicals; in other words we all have a unique pheromonic odour.

Many researchers in this field are now certain that the degree of sexual harmony, or lack of it, between a couple is very powerfully influenced by their level of pheromonic compatibility. So in some cases conflicts in a relationship may be based on chemical incompatibility, and therefore be unresolvable.

Indeed, if the 'chemistry' between a couple is not right, no amount of compatibility in terms of personality, interests and behaviour will ever be able to produce that genuine, romantic, sexually exciting love everyone is looking for. You might love many things in a person, but if this physical-chemical attraction is not there, you may well find that what you have is a very good friend, but not a sexually satisfying romance.

Before applying this compatibility assessment procedure, you should first refer to the chapters 'This Has Never Happened To Me Before!', 'I Could Never Do This With My Partner!', 'I Wonder...Straight or Gay?' and 'The Sublimated Lover'. If one or both samples falls into any of these categories, there will undoubtedly be significant sexual problems in the relationship, and under such circumstances you may wish to omit the following assessment procedure.

Once the assessment procedure in this chapter is complete you should also check two other chapters: 'Foreplay? Who Cares?' and 'Are You In Danger?'

ASSESSING COMPATIBILITY OF RAW SEXUAL ENERGY/DESIRE

To graphologically assess sexual compatibility between a couple is incredibly straightforward and simple and the whole process should not take you more than a few minutes for each writing sample. You do, however, need to go through several important, easy-to-follow steps. With one of the samples of writing in front of you, carry out the following procedure:

1. Look at the letter 'g's in the writing sample and measure

the stem length of the two longest ones as shown in the example below.

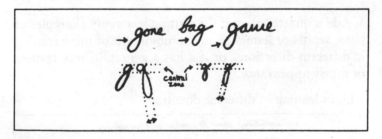

(As you can see, the object here is to estimate how long the descending line is in comparison with the height of the central zone.) Having done this, take the average of these two stem lengths and write down the result (e.g. if one descending line measures three and a half times the height of the central zone and the other is four and a half, then your score will be four). Your present score can now be increased if any of the following apply:

2. Add half a point if the writing has two or more 'g's with a looped stem that is at least as wide as the central zone (see example below). If, however, the looped stems are twice (or more) as wide as the central zone, add one whole point.

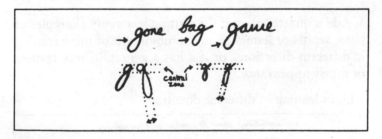

3. Add half a point if the pressure of the writing on the paper is so heavy that it makes indentations, clearly showing on the reverse of the paper. If, however, the lower stems have a faded appearance indicative of weak pressure, then do not add this half point.

4. Add half a point if the writing has one (or more) of the following three characteristics:

• Writing containing many letters that are clogged with ink.

> *George and Kathy have come*

• Writing which has a muddy, smudgy or smeary appearance.

> *The unending joys of sexuality are here.*

• Writing done from choice with a thick felt-tip pen, or any other pen producing broad, thick lines.

> **feelings Awareness**

5. Add a quarter point if the writing has many examples of lines, words or letters or any combination of these leaning in different directions, or if it has a generally very restless or messy appearance.

• Lines leaning in different directions.

> *my emotions seem to control me completely at other times I just feel detached from it all.*

• Words leaning in different directions.

> *attitudes change moment to moment*

• Letters leaning in different directions.

feel so inwardly restless

6. Add a quarter point if the writing noticeably leans to the right (at least as much as in the sample shown below).

Understanding feelings

The score you now have is your final score for the piece of writing you have in front of you. Having recorded this score, apply the same procedure to the other writing sample, so that you have in front of you a score for each person.

A glance at the following interpretations will allow you to instantly translate a person's score, in terms of the strength of their sexual energy and desire. The higher the score, the stronger their sexual energy and desire for sex. People with very low scores will desire sex only infrequently and when they do make love, once will almost always be enough. Those who have strong sexual energy need frequent sex to feel satisfied, and will feel very frustrated with any partner who denies them very regular sex.

Below one and a half points = sexual difficulties. This score signifies poor physical stamina, combined with a very low sex drive. These types can accept going without sex for long periods of time, and there is a fair chance that someone in this category will occasionally suffer from problems of impotence or frigidity.

One and a half to two points = low sexual energy/desire. These people have a lower than average level of physical stamina and a sex drive that is also below the norm. Making love once a week will usually be enough for most people whose writing falls into this category.

Two and a half to three points = average sexual energy/ desire. People with this score are average in terms of physical stamina and sexual energy. Sexually not particularly demanding, most individuals in this group will not complain if they make love only a couple of times a week, and they will rarely, if ever, need or want a repeat performance in the same session.

Three and a half to four points = strong sexual energy/ desire. These are healthy, robust people with plenty of physical/sexual stamina and a well above average desire for lovemaking. The majority of individuals in this category will need and expect to make love three or four times a week, every week of the year, and they are bound occasionally to need to make love more than once in the same session. They will feel very frustrated if their partner has a low sex drive.

Four and a half to five and a half points = extremely strong sexual energy/desire. These types are simply overflowing with abundant physical and sexual energy and, except in very rare cases where this energy has been suppressed or sublimated for some reason, people in this group will require sex almost on a daily basis, all the year round (unless they burn off vast amounts of energy in daily exercise). It is by no means unusual for such individuals to require repeat performances during the same lovemaking session, in order to try to satisfy their often insatiable sexual appetites.

Above six points = excessive sexual energy/desire. The majority of these individuals are simply exploding with an excessive amount of physical stamina and sexual desire. All the attributes connected with the previous category are amplified here. Sex every day is essential for their peace of mind, unless they are sports fanatics who are channelling large portions of their energy into physical activity. These types are especially prone to infidelity if living with a low sex drive partner, as they cannot tolerate the build-up of sexual frustration in such circumstances.

ASSESSING THE DEGREE OF COMPATIBILITY BETWEEN A COUPLE'S SCORES

(Please note that couples who both have scores below one and a half points are likely to have difficulties in the sexual sphere of the relationship due to possible sexual problems.)

Couples with identical scores, or only a half point difference = fantastic sexual compatibility.
With this degree of sexual compatibility a couple should be able to resolve any areas of conflict that may exist elsewhere in the relationship, in particular in the areas discussed later on in this section. This couple will have matching amounts of sexual energy and will have the same frequency of desire for sex. (If the scores are above six, however, some couples in this category may need to guard against a mutual tendency for promiscuous behaviour.)

Couples with a one point difference in scores = adequate sexual compatibility.
This couple, however, will definitely notice some difference in the frequency of their desire for sex. The partner with the higher score is therefore likely to occasionally feel a little sexually frustrated.

Couples with a one and a half point score difference = resolvable sexual incompatibility.
There will be a very noticeable sexual desire discrepancy between these two, but as long as there are no major incompatibilities in the other areas described in this section, this conflict should be resolvable if the couple is prepared to discuss the situation openly. With major incompatibilities in any of the areas described in the chapters that follow, severe conflicts could develop that will need the assistance of a professional sex therapist.

Couples with a two point score difference = serious sexual incompatibility.
The partner with the higher score is likely to feel extremely sexually frustrated on a regular basis (unless of course he or she is sublimating sexual energy via other channels). If there is also incompatibility in any of the areas described later, the problems will be greatly exacerbated, and professional therapeutic guidance will almost definitely be needed to resolve the problem.

Couples with a two and a half point difference or more = severe sexual incompatibility.
Professional therapeutic help is definitely needed. If there are also incompatibilities in more than one of the areas that follow, there may well be severe and unresolvable differences between the couple.

The following areas also play a role in determining the quality of a couple's sex life and their level of sexual compatibility. But if two people are sexually very compatible according to the above categories, then they should be able to resolve any conflicts that could arise in the relationship if there are incompatibilities in any of these areas.

31. Assessing Emotional Compatibility

You can predict probable incompatibility between two people if their emotional make-up is poorly matched. If a couple's handwriting fits the description of any of the categories below, there is a strong chance that there will be conflicts in communication stemming from emotional disharmony, which may negatively affect many areas of their relationship, including their sex life (even if their writing indicates they are potentially highly compatible in terms of their sexual appetites). If none of the categories below are applicable, then one can deduce that there will be no significant problems in communication at this level of the relationship.

Emotional incompatibility is likely if:

a. One or both of the partners in the relationship has writing (of any style) that leans extremely far to the left, as much or more to the left as in the writing samples below:

> to keep my emotions private
>
> feelings are difficult to express
>
> *rarely live up fully to ones original expectations*

This extreme leftward-leaning writing denotes an emotionally over-controlled, severely disturbed nature, and no matter what type of emotional make-up the other partner may have, there is bound to be disharmony in the emotional zone of the relationship.

b. One of the partners in the relationship has writing (of any style) which leans gently, but noticeably, to the left, as much or more to the left as in the writing samples shown below:

> *sometimes overcontrolled .*
>
> *holding in ones feelings at times*

and the other partner has writing (of any style) which leans gently, but noticeably, to the right, as much or more to the right as in the writing sample shown below:

> *smoothly expressed feelings*
>
> *needing to show emotion*

In this relationship there will be conflict, because the partner whose writing leans to the right will find his or her mate emotionally undemonstrative and often lacking in warmth.

c. One of the partners in the relationship has writing (of any style) which is essentially vertical in appearance (or extremely near to vertical)

> *the head should always control the heart*
>
> *emotional control allows for balance*

and the other partner has writing (of any style) which leans quite strongly to the right, as much or more as in the sample below:

> *Understanding feelings*

There will be a conflict of emotions in this case, because the person with vertical writing is liable to consider his or her mate over-emotional as well as moody, subjective and irrational at times, and the partner with strongly rightward-leaning writing will find the other irritatingly pragmatic, emotionally reserved and insufficiently affectionate.

d. One or both of the partners in the relationship has writing (of any style) that leans extremely far to the right, as much or more to the right as in the writing samples shown below:

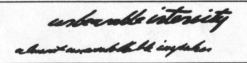

This extreme rightward-leaning writing denotes an excessively over-emotional, highly neurotic nature that is prone to hysterical outbursts when under pressure. No matter what type of emotional make-up such a person's partner may have, there is still bound to be emotional disharmony in the relationship.

32. Assessing Sexual Imagination and Openness

If there is a significant imbalance between a couple in terms of their sexual openness and imagination, this can be a source of conflict in the relationship that can significantly reduce the pleasure they gain from lovemaking.

A mis-match in the area of sexual imagination and openness is likely if:

One of the partners in the relationship has handwriting (of any style) containing several examples of 'g's with balloon-shaped stems reaching the baseline, which are at least as wide as the central zone, as shown in the example below:

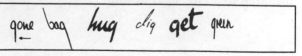

and the other partner has writing (of any style) in which the 'g's consistently have any of the following types of stem, or any combination of these stems:

a. Only a descending line.

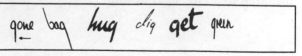

b. Like the small letter 'q'.

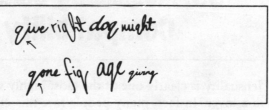

c. Ascending line completed, but remaining far below the central zone.

d. Looped stem which is very narrow in appearance (as narrow or narrower than in the examples below):

e. End of stem is sharply angled.

If a couple's writing reveals an imbalance in terms of sexual imagination, the partner with the vivid imagination is likely rapidly to tire of his or her mate's routine, unimaginative sexual behaviour patterns, and will probably feel that the style of foreplay and approach to lovemaking is rather unspontaneous and uninspiring. It would be advisable for this couple to discuss the problem openly.

317

33. Assessing Sensual Compatibility

Sensuality is clearly one of the most highly valued features in a lover. In fact, many people rate this characteristic as more important than sexual stamina.

Someone who revels in every inch of his or her lover's body, who does not just go through the motions in a half-hearted manner is liable to be regarded by many individuals as a better lover than someone who may have a much better body and far more sexual endurance, but who lacks sensuality. There will be a noticeable sexual incompatibility between two individuals if one of them has a strongly sensual nature while the other has an ascetic or very unsensual nature. The areas in between these two extremes are not so important, as milder degrees of incompatibility should not pose too much of a problem if there is a fair degree of sexual harmony elsewhere.

Sensual incompatibility is likely if:

One of the partners uses by choice a pen that has an extremely fine tip that produces sharp writing.

Learn control over the baser instincts

and the other has writing which has one (or more) of the following three characteristics:

- Writing containing many letters that are clogged with ink.

> *George and Cathy have come*

- Writing which has a muddy, smudgy or smeary appearance.

> *The unending joys of Sensuality are here.*

- Writing done from choice with a thick felt-tip pen, or any other pen producing broad, thick lines.

> **feelings Awareness**

If there is an incompatibility in this area, then the partner who is sensual is likely to feel deprived of sufficient physically expressed warmth and affection, and will be very discontented with the other's style of foreplay and lovemaking, which will seem to lack any real passion or sensitivity.

Appendix

THE HISTORICAL EVOLUTION OF HANDWRITING ANALYSIS

No one really knows when the art/science of analyzing writing actually began.

Although the modern techniques of handwriting analysis used by today's graphologists have evolved over a fairly short period of time, the awareness or intuition of the close link between writing and personality stretches back into antiquity. Indeed, the oldest known reference to the subject appears in an ancient Hindu manuscript written in the Sanskrit language over five thousand years ago that discusses various techniques for interpreting writing as a means of discovering character.

There are records from the Middle Ages suggesting that handwriting analysis was practised to some extent in European monasteries, and during the Renaissance it caught the attention of Michelangelo, and of Shakespeare, who stated, 'Give me the handwriting of a woman and I will tell you her character.' The explorer Sir Walter Raleigh is also credited with making statements expressing his belief in the highly revealing nature of a person's script.

It was in 1622 that the first serious book on the subject was published, and it attracted little interest. In 1872, however, a French clergyman, Abbé Jean-Hippolyte Michon, published a book on handwriting analysis based on many years of studious research, and the popularity of this work established him as the father of the subject. It was he who coined the word 'graphology', derived from a synthesis of two Greek words: 'graphein', meaning both 'writing' and 'drawing', and 'logos' which can be freely interpreted as 'the science of'.

Two key figures of interest who later contributed to the growing popularity of this subject were Goethe and his friend Johann Kasper Lavater, the Swiss poet, physiognomist and theologian. An extensive correspondence began between them on the subject of handwriting analysis, and this was later published. In one letter Goethe wrote, 'There does not exist the shadow of a doubt that handwriting has its analogies with the character and with the human mind...'

In America, Edgar Allan Poe was so fascinated by the subject of handwriting analysis that he not only spent much time analyzing script but his results were published in 1926, more than seventy years after his death.

The artist Thomas Gainsborough, when he painted someone's portrait, liked to keep a sample of their handwriting on the easel in front of him, in order to help tap into the real essence of his sitter's personality.

The brilliant analytical mind of Sir Arthur Conan Doyle was also drawn to this subject, as was the French master of story-telling Guy de Maupassant, who revealed his great respect for this field with his words, 'Dark words on white paper bare the soul.' Disraeli stated that, 'Handwriting bears an analogy to the character of the writer...' Albert Schweitzer, the medical missionary and philosopher who received the Nobel Peace Prize in 1952, believed deeply in the validity of graphology and was himself a member of the Société de Graphologie de Paris. Other renowned figures who held handwriting analysis in great esteem include Baudelaire, Balzac, Anton Chekhov, Robert Browning and his wife Elizabeth Barrett Browning, Charles Dickens, Alexandre Dumas *fils*, Alphonse Daudet, Gogol, Thomas Mann, Mendelssohn, George Sand, Madame de Stael,

Verlaine and Emile Zola.

In France, a book on handwriting analysis was written by Alphonse Bertillon, who appeared as one of the expert handwriting analysts in the trial of Captain Alfred Dreyfus in 1899 and, at around the same time in England, another eminent figure, Sir William Herschel, the pioneer of fingerprint testing, began to take an interest in graphology. He stated his belief that graphology was as important in personality assessment as he predicted fingerprint identification would be to criminology.

In France, at the Sorbonne, the father of intelligence testing, Alfred Binet, tested the assumption that specific character traits correlate with specific handwriting traits, and he achieved affirmative results with respect to the graphic indices of honesty and intelligence.

In Germany, Dr Ludwig Klages, the 'high priest' of the German school of graphology, wrote a famous text on handwriting analysis entitled *Handschrift und Charakter (Writing and Personality)*. In 1929 the thirteenth printing of this book became a standard text in the psychology departments of German universities, even in preference to the works of Sigmund Freud. Klages played a key role in establishing graphology as a valid branch of scientific research. Half a century later, Albert Einstein indicated his regard for the subject of handwriting analysis when he wrote, 'Graphology has always interested me, although I have as yet not made a systematic study of it.'

Sigmund Freud clearly saw the potential of graphology, as is evident from his comment, 'There is no doubt that men express their character through their handwriting.' Dr Alfred Adler, the Viennese psychologist, also had a great deal of respect for the subject, and referred to it frequently, stating on one occasion, 'Handwriting is frozen motion.'

Jung, too, acknowledged the relevance of handwriting

analysis. A well-known graphologist, Anne Teillard, who was a student of Jung for more than thirty years, expanded the use of Jungian depth psychology in handwriting, with the help of his personal guidance.

The considerable effort directed towards the study of graphology by numerous European and American researchers has now finally established graphology as an integral part of psychological and personality assessment procedures all over the world.

Bibliography

GRAPHOLOGY

Amend, Karen Kristen & Ruiz, Mary Stansbury
Achieving Compatibility with Handwriting Analysis,
Volumes 1 & 2, Newcastle Publishing Co Inc, 1992

Bernard, Marie
Sexual Deviations, The Whitstone Publishing Company,
1990

Falcon, Hal, PhD
How to Analyse Handwriting, Trident Press, 1964

Holt, Arthur (Doctor of Jurisprudence)
Handwriting in Psychological Interpretation, Charles C.
Thomas, 1965, 1974

Klages, Dr Ludwig
Handschrift und Charakter, Verlag Von Johann
Ambrosius Barth, 1921

Marcuse, Irene, PhD
Guide to Personality Through Handwriting, Arco
Publishing Company Inc, 1974

Roman, Klara, PhD
*The Encyclopaedia of the Written Word – A Lexicon for
Graphology and Other Aspects of Writing*, Frederick
Ungor Publishing Company, 1968

324

Sonnemann, Ulrich, PhD
Handwriting Analysis as a Psychodiagnostic Tool, Grune
and Stratton Inc, 1950

Victor, Frank, PhD
Handwriting, A Personality Projection, Charles C.
Thomas, 1952

Wolff, Werner, PhD
*Diagrams of the Unconscious – Handwriting and
Personality in Measurement, Experiment and Analysis*,
Grune and Stratton Inc, 1948

PSYCHOLOGY AND RELATED SUBJECTS

Adler, Alfred
*Understanding Human Nature & What Life Could Mean
To You*, Oneworld Publications Ltd, 1992

Benson, Herbert, MD with Klipper, Miriam Z.
The Relaxation Response, Avon Books, 1976

Comfort, Alex, MB PhD (editor)
The Joy of Sex, Quartet Books Ltd, 1980

Jampolsky, Gerald G, MD
Love is Letting Go of Fear, Bantam Books, 1985

Moir, Anne, PhD & Jessel, David
Brainsex, The Real Difference Between Men and Women,
Mandarin Paperbacks, 1993

Rogers, Julie, PhD
Understanding People, Nelson-Hall Inc, 1979

Swami Rama, Ballentine, Rudolph, MD, Swami Ajaya, PhD
Yoga and Psychotherapy, The Evolution of Consciousness, The Himalayan International Institute of Yoga Science and Philosophy, 1981

Selye, Hans, MD
The Stress of Life, McGraw-Hill Book Co, 1984

Stanway, Andrew, Consultant Dr
The Loving Touch, A Guide to Being a Better Lover, Macdonald & Co (Publishers) Ltd, 1990

Wilson, Glenn, Consultant Dr
The Intimate Touch, A Guide To More Active Lovemaking For You And Your Partner and *The Sensual Touch, A Guide To More Exotic Lovemaking*, Macdonald & Co (Publishers) Ltd, 1990